CW01632083

Susan McGowan studied at the Dorset Institute of Higher Education before being awarded a BA at Southampton University. After almost a decade as an Internal Auditor in the Civil Service, and twenty years as a school librarian, Susan now lives in Kent and devotes her time to reading, researching and writing.

Literary Kent

a personal choice of 50 writers

influenced by the county of Kent

Susan McGowan

Literary Kent

ISBN 978-1-9999321-5-2

Contents

Introduction

How many authors have been born in, found themselves inspired by, travelled through or came to live in, the county of Kent? The answer is hundreds – from those who merely passed through to reach continental Europe to those born and bred here, who would consider themselves Kentish to the core.

This book is a selection of some well-known and some lesser-known authors who have visited the county with pen and paper and felt moved to jot down a few words.

Some readers may wonder that I have not included their own favourites – where is Anthony Buckeridge, creator of JCT Jennings, who taught at St Lawrence College in Ramsgate, Julie Wassmer, whose *Whitstable Pearl* mysteries are set on the north coast of the county, Wilbert Awdry, writer of *Thomas the Tank Engine* or Frank Muir, self-confessed *Kentish Lad?*

The reason is that there just isn't enough room for them all. Edmund Spencer, who wrote part of *The Faerie Queen* at Penshurst is missing, as is Lewis Carol who was struck by the wonder of the Shell Grotto in Margate. Oscar Wilde, George Bernard Shaw, Frederick Forsyth and Clive King have all been influenced by Kent. I have read these authors and admire their works, but this little book is my personal choice of a few writers whose stories have inspired me.

Kent has provided much to the literary history of our nation and I proudly present this select group of writers, showing their particular connections with the county.

Susan

St Peters Church, Sandwich

1

Matthew Arnold

(1822-1888)

Arnold was a prolific writer of essays and poetry, often adopting a note of reprimand in his works, leaning very much towards the Victorian idea that literature should instruct rather than entertain.

His poem 'Dover Beach' was written after two brief visits to the town – one when he passed through on his way to the continent with his new wife in the summer of 1851 and the other on his return in October.

“Only, from the long line of spray
Where the sea meets the moon-blanched land,
Listen! you hear the grating roar
Of pebbles which the waves draw back, and fling,
At their return, up the high strand,
Begin, and cease, and then again begin,
With tremulous cadence slow, and bring
The eternal note of sadness in.”

The poem reflects on the passage of time, and the rise and fall of nations, and how a sense of belonging is formed. Arnold was not yet 30 when he wrote the poem, and although he was on his honeymoon, the poem strikes a melancholy note, almost seeming to be a portent of doom rather than a herald of the future.

2

Jane Austen

(1775-1817)

Jane Austen was neither a Kentish Maid nor a Maid of Kent, but she had many acquaintances in the county, and made frequent visits throughout her lifetime. Although some of her letters are lost, plenty still remain and they give a fascinating insight into her time with us.

The writer was just twelve when she first came to Kent, travelling to Sevenoaks with her sister to stay at The Red House, now No. 50 High Street, with her uncle. Her father had been born in Tonbridge, and many of her family still lived nearby.

As a boy, Austen's brother Edward had been adopted by the wealthy Knight family, who owned Godmersham Park, lying half-way between Canterbury and Ashford and after his marriage, he moved to Rowling House to be near his in-laws who lived at Goodnestone Park. When Austen came to Kent, she enjoyed the beautiful countryside exercising for pleasure as well as when travelling. One visit she paid during her stay was to Nackington, some 10 miles from Rowling, where she dined with the Milles family, returning by moonlight.

When his in-laws died, Edward inherited the property at Godmersham and Jane and her sister Cassandra stayed with them frequently. It was here that she started to write *First Impressions*, a book she later retitled *Pride and Prejudice*. The way of life was very different from her economical way of living at home and she writes to her sister Cassandra in 1798 "Kent is the only place for happiness; everybody is rich there."

An interesting note about the Godmersham letters, both to and from the house, is that they were generally addressed to 'Godmersham, Canterbury'. With the address 'Godmersham, Faversham', the letters would have gone to the Faversham office from where they could be collected; those coming into Canterbury would have been delivered to the house. Although this cost an extra penny on the postage, it seems that it was worth the expense.

Godmersham gained national fame when it was included on the Bank of England £10 note along Austen' portrait in 2017, beating many of the other locations associated with the author. The house is generally agreed to be the basis for Mansfield Park in the book of the same name, and parts of the novel may even have been written during one of her stays in Kent.

In 1796 there is a tantalizing letter from Austen to her sister discussing an outing to Greenwich, at that time in Kent. Sadly, we have no more details than her intention to go there.

While travelling to and from Hampshire, Austen usually stayed at The Bull & George in Dartford. On her way home from a holiday in October 1798, she writes to her sister from inn, telling her that “it wanted five minutes of twelve when we left Sittingbourne, from whence we had a famous pair of horses, which took us to Rochester in an hour and a quarter; the postboy seemed determined to show my mother that Kentish drivers were not always tedious and really drove as fast as Cax."(generally agreed to be the name of a coach firm local to the Austens). However, the next leg of their journey was slower as “the road was heavy and our horses very indifferent”. It was past four when they arrived at the inn.

They dined at a little after five, but not before an event which must have startled Austen considerably. Her writing and dressing boxes had been accidentally loaded onto the chaise for Gravesend, in with other luggage bound for The West Indies. Luckily someone noticed the error and before long a man was dispatched on a fast horse to catch the chaise and return the boxes.

The writer Samuel Egerton Brydges recorded seeing Austen in Ramsgate in 1803. She would have been visiting her brother, Captain Francis Austen, who at the age of 29 had been tasked with leading the Sea Fencibles to defend that part of the Kentish coast. Tens of thousands of troops moved through the port, travelling to and from the continent, and the town was regularly full of soldiers. Austen may have joined the crowds as they watched the troop exercises that took place on the sands.

In 1808 she remembered Ramsgate when she wrote the poem '*See they Come, Post Haste from Thanet*' for her niece, to celebrate the marriage of her brother Francis.

> 'Canterbury they have passed through;
> Next succeeded Stamford-bridge;
> Chilham village they came fast through;
> Now they've mounted yonder ridge.
> Down the hill they're swift proceeding,
> Now they skirt the Park around;'

Kentish-dwellers will know that Stamford Bridge is not located between Canterbury and Chilham and realise that Austen, of course, means Shalmsford Bridge.

Shalmsford Bridge, Chartham

Many academics cite Ramsgate as the inspiration for *Sanditon*, a town in the novel of the same name which stood between two cliffs, as does Ramsgate. Austen certainly liked being by the sea, although she was ambivalent about sea-bathing, which was a new craze sweeping the nation at the time.

In 1805 she was once more in Kent, and stayed at Goodnestone Farm. She commented: "We have walked to Rowling on each of the two last days after dinner, and very great was my pleasure in going over the house and grounds". Using local footpaths, the distance would have been less than two miles – an easy stroll for those used to walking.

Austen also stayed briefly at Eastwell manor, home of the Finch-Hatton family. Austen was offered the use of the family hairdresser before one event, and again before a ball at the Ashford assembly rooms at The Saracen's Head Family Hotel and Posting House, which was just over 6 miles from Godmerhsam Park. The building once stood on the corner between North Street and The High Street, but has now been demolished in favour of a Sainsbury's supermarket. On each occasion, she was charged a nominal fee by the hairdresser, who was apparently aware of her straightened circumstances.

Her letters indicate that Austen was not particularly fond of the balls, but none-the-less continued to attend, out of politeness and also, presumably, to gather details of such social occasions for her books. We know that she attended one in Deal, in 1805, at the Assembly Rooms on the corner of Duke Street. Cassandra was not in Kent on this occasion, and so Austen writes to her about the evening.

A further trip to Godmersham came in 1808. She left Dartford at 10.30am, after stopping once again at The Bull & George for breakfast, “the same inn at which we breakfasted in that said journey, and on the present occasion had about the same bad butter”. The party reached The George at Sittingbourne at 3pm noting that “a few minutes, of course, did for Sittingbourne” and finally arrived at Godmersham at 6pm.

A typical day at Godmersham is described by Austen in a letter to her sister.

> “Yesterday passed quite à la Godmersham: the gentlemen rode about Edward's farm, and returned in time to saunter along Bentigh with us; and after dinner we visited the Temple Plantations, which, to be sure, is a Chevalier Bayard of a plantation. James and Mary are much struck with the beauty of the place. To-day the spirit of the thing is kept up by the two brothers being gone to Canterbury in the chair.”

‘Temple Plantations’ refers to the area of woodland known as Palmtree Hill Plantation at Temple Ewell near Dover.

She also described one of her own trips to Canterbury, where she walked with a friend to call on the elderly Mrs Bridges, while others in the party went to see an acquaintance who lived in the houses within the cathedral precincts. Austen may have also met Miss Milles near the cathedral, as it is speculated that it is she who was the inspiration for Miss Bates in *Emma*.

The day was a busy one, but Austen found time to call on her brother’s adoptive mother, Mrs Knight, who lived at The White Friars in Canterbury. The estate, now the site of The White Friars Shopping Centre, was the home of Sir Henry Finch and his family. She was invited to stay overnight to meet Mr & Mrs Natchbull, and travelled there with a friend one day, to be collected by her brother Edward the next evening. Reading between the lines, it seems that Mrs Knight was kind enough as to give Austen a regular allowance.

Travelling through Kent later the same year, Austen wrote "I shall be sorry to pass the door at Seale without calling but it must be so". Seale, near Sevenoaks, was the home to George Austen's half-brother William Walter and his family.

In 1809, Austen was once again in the county and spent a day in Dover. Afterwards the group attended a fair in Fredville, near Godmersham, where she dined with and sometimes stayed with politician John Plumptre and his family. Her letters mention several trips into Canterbury, both to shop and to dine with friends. Neither the A28 nor the A2 had been built at that time, so the party would have travelled through Chartham and Thanington Without, entering the city via Wincheap.

In 1813, Austen was once seeing friends in Kent, dining with family and, of course, shopping. Fanny Knight, Austen's niece writes that she went with 'Aunt Jane' and her father to Wrotham to dine with Mr and Mrs Moore, "waiting some time at Lenham". She also visited the Rev Sir John Fagge, rector of St Mary's at Chartham who lived at Mystole Place. "I was surprised to find Mystole so pretty," she writes. The red-brick house has now been altered, with the addition of many more windows and dormers, and has been divided into apartments, but is in an enviable position now designated an Area of Outstanding Natural Beauty.

In her description of one trip to Mystole, Austen mentions that

> "Our gentlemen are all gone to their Sittingbourne meeting, East and West Kent, in one barouche together -- rather, West Kent driving East Kent. I believe that is not the usual way of the county."

What an intriguing example of the age-old rivalry between East and West Kent!

Austen also travelled east, and attended The Canterbury Ball the same year, where there was 'good company but no dancing'. Another trip to Canterbury was undertaken when her brother, a Magistrate, was required to inspect the gaol, situated in The Westgate Towers. Austen went with him, but "went through all the feelings which People must go through I think in visiting such a Building". It is tempting to think that she ascended the narrow staircase to the roof of the tower, where she would have had a fine view of the city. She notes that she bought a sprig of flowers 'for her old age'. Research into the language of flowers reveals that the message of Michaelmas daisies is 'joy in old age', so we assume that it was the flowers we now refer to as asters that she bought.

Austen's brother Henry is buried in the Woodbury Park Cemetery in Tunbridge Wells, and the town is mentioned several times in her novels.

3

RM Ballantyne

(1825-1894)

Robert Michael Ballantyne was born in Edinburgh, and wrote books with strong, moral characters at their heart. His works were based on experience, or at the very least exhaustive research. He was a prolific writer, and completed over 100 books in his lifetime, the best-known of which are *The Coral Island* and *The Lifeboat.*

As a young man, the writer spent six years in Canada working for the Hudson Bay Company. He then returned to Scotland and worked in various other industries before concentrating on his writing from the age of about 30, using these experiences as the basis for many of his books.

As part of his research for *The Lighthouse* (1864), Ballantyne spent three weeks on a lighthouse off the coast of Arbroath. He also worked as a fireman on the London-Edinburgh steam train, which brought him to the south of the country.

Travelling through Kent, Ballantyne ended up in the far eastern corner of the country, once again battling the sea. He spent time on The Gull lightship and spoke to fishermen all along the eastern Kent coast, whose reminiscences he used in *The Lifeboat (*1864).

The memories of his time on The Gull eventually became *The Floating Light of the Goodwin Sands* (1870), which contains the lines:

> 'Oh, Ramsgate, where in all the earth
> Beside the lovely sea
> Can any town of note or worth
> Be found equal to thee?'

He was grateful to the Ramsgate men who helped him, and thanked them in the acknowledgements of the book.

> 'My best thanks, for much useful information, are due to Mr Isaac Jarman, the coxswain, and Mr Fish, the bowman, of the Ramsgate Lifeboat-men who may be said to carry their lives continually in their hands, and whose profession it is to go out at the call of duty and systematically grapple with Death and rob him of his prey. To the Harbour Master and Deputy Harbour Master at Ramsgate, I am also indebted for information and assistance, and to Mr Reading, the master of the Aid

steam-tug, which attends upon and shares the perils of, the Lifeboat.'

The steam-tug was used to tow the lifeboat towards a stricken vessel so the crew could effect a rescue and to keep towing it back into position as the winds and storm currents moved it. This could not have been accomplished by oar-power alone.

A further description of a Ramsgate lifeboat can be found in *Man on the Ocean A Book About Boats and Ships* which reproduces a letter sent by Ballantyne in 1870 after he spent a week on The Gull lightship and witnessed a real-life lifeboat call-out.

Although is books were intended for a juvenile audience, and were conceived as adventure books for boys, the modern historian can tease out a wealth of information from the pages, and create for themselves a picture of life in the early 19th century. One has only to stand on The Harbour Arm during rough weather to appreciate the bravery of the lifeboat men of Kent.

4

Richard H Barham

(1788-1845)

Richard Harris Barham created a whole series of fantastical legends – in verse! – set in the county of Kent. He wrote under the pseudonym Thomas Ingoldsby of Tappington Manor and called his book *The Ingoldsby Legends*, after their supposed collector.

Barham was born at 61 Burgate, Canterbury, just within the city walls and close to the cathedral. The house has long since gone, but a blue plaque marks the spot, and on a busy market day, it is possible to get a sense of the bustling thoroughfare. Richard's father died when he was just seven years old, and he inherited the huge, rambling house known as Tappington Everard, near Denton, which he immortalised as Tappington Manor, mixed with a little knowledge of nearby Broome Park and more than a smattering of artistic licence. The manor house is surrounded by Tappington Moor, or as we know it, Barham Downs, which features in the legend *Hand of Glory*. The area is low, with arching skies and rolling hills, beautiful in summer, but bitterly cold in winter, akin to the wuthering moors of Yorkshire or the spreading moorland of Wessex.

Barham became the Rector of Snargate and Curate of Warehorne, where he lived for three years before he moved permanently to London. Although he loved the Kentish countryside, the comforts of London held many more attractions for him.

The Ingoldsby Legends were set in the medieval era and were serialised in Mr Bentley's Miscellany between 1837 and 1844. This monthly magazine was produced from 1836-1868, and is remembered for the fact that it was edited by Charles Dickens for the first two years. Dickens would have been familiar with the work of Mr Richard Barham.

The stories in *The Ingoldsby Legends* purport to be traditional Kentish tales, but while many of them draw on local folklore, just as many are purely from Barham's own imagination. His premise was that Thomas Ingoldsby of Tappington Manor had inherited a trunk full of antique manuscripts, and that his stories are a distillation of those tales.

Barham stayed in Margate several times from 1837, travelling by steam packet from London (a journey of seven hours). In 1841 he records the journey and his subsequent arrival in Margate as a farcical event, made amusing by his evident good humour. He liked to stay at 20 The Parade, a house subsequently named Ingoldsby House. The frontage was altered following subsidence, but a blue plaque has nonetheless been erected to mark the location.

In *The Leech of Folkestone* it was Barham who first brought forth the idea that Romney Marsh could be considered as The Fifth Continent, due to the striking nature of its own particular character. He said '... according to the best geographers the world is divided into Europe, Asia, Africa, America and Romney Marsh.' This identification struck a chord with the locals and the assertion has persisted ever since.

The Ingoldsby Legends cover the whole of Kent, from *The Grey Dolphin* of Sheppey to *The Lay of the Old Woman Clothed in Grey* of Dover and from *Misadventures in Margate* to *Jerry Jarvis's Wig: a Legend of The Weald of Kent*. Setting his tales in recognisable places gives them credence and many are retold as ancient legends rather than Victorian fiction. Visitors to Canterbury, for example, can see *The Dark Entry*, a passageway joining Green Court to Canterbury Cathedral which features in the story of Nell Cook, who was implicated in a plot to poison her employer and his lover. Her punishment was to be buried alive under the flagstones, and her ghost is said to walk on Friday evenings.

Wherever you go in the county, you will never be far from the site of an Ingoldsby legend and they continue to influence story-tellers and novelists to this day.

5

HE Bates

(1905-1974)

Herbert Ernest Bates lived for over 40 years in Little Chart Forstal near Tenterden, and created some of the most endearing and enduring Kentish characters in literature, writing light fiction such as *The Darling Buds of May* as well as deeper works such as *Love for Lydia.*

Bates and his wife bought The Granary, as it was known, in 1931, which stood in half an acre of land, near enough to the village green to be central to village life, but secluded enough to allow him some privacy. Originally a grain store, the house was enlarged and the gardens landscaped to make an idyllic home for the whole family. Bates was a keen gardener, and wrote several books on the subject.

His first Kentish work of fiction, *The Darling Buds of May*, was written in 1958 and tells the story of the Larkins. Legend has it that Herbert used his observations of a real family as the basis for the Larkins, having seen them buying picnic supplies at a corner shop in Faversham. Using his initial notes, combined with his recollections, the group morphed into the Larkin family we know and love today.

The Larkins are loud and generous, taking life as they find it and enjoying the ride. They live a hand-to-mouth existence selling scrap and other oddments, or picking fruit in season. Money is spent as soon as it comes into the house, and they enjoy a series of misadventures throughout the books, set against a background of merriment and mutual affection.

The TV series from the 1990s was filmed in Pluckley and the countryside around it, and will still be recognisable to avid Larkin fans. The Larkin farm, Home Farm, was filmed at Buss Farm, just south of the village, which has now been renamed Darling Buds Farm.

Many of the other locations used in the series would have been familiar to the Bates, and are more than likely the original inspiration for the places in the Larkin books. The Kent & East Sussex Railway was used several times, and the Shepherd Neame Brewery in Faversham became Bristow's Brewery. The Larkins can be seen picnicking on the south coast of Kent at Folkestone beach and also strolling along Folkestone Harbour.

As well as five Larkin books, Bates wrote a series of novels based on his war experiences, and several books for children.

Alongside this work, he wrote under the pen-name Flying Officer X for the RAF's wartime public relations department, a valuable addition to the war effort.

Bates died in 1974, aged 68, and is buried in the Kent County Crematorium at Charing, where there is a memorial urn and a plaque.

A Kentish oast house

6

Aphra Behn

(1640-1689)

The inspirational female writier Aphra Johnson was born in mid-Kent during the reign of Charles I, in either Harbledown, just outside Canterbury or in Wye – scholars have yet to agree on the exact location.

Before she reached her teenage years, the King was dead, the monarchy had been ousted and England was ruled by Parliament as a Commonwealth. By the time she was 20, the monarchy had been restored to the Stuart dynasty and Charles II was on the throne. Interesting times indeed!

Soon after this, Behn's father was appointed to a military post in Suriname, and the family went to live in South American for several years. It was here that Behn found inspiration for her later novel, *Oroonoko (1688)*.

In the early 1660s, Behn married a Dutch merchant and took his name, becoming Aphra Behn, and they probably moved to The Spanish Netherlands (now part of Belgium). Sadly, Behn was soon widowed and needed to find a means of supporting herself.

She turned to writing, but also found herself engaged in espionage activities, working in Antwerp as a spy for the newly-restored King Charles II, under the code name Astrea. She was one of the few people to warn of the Dutch raid on the River Medway in 1667.

Less than ten years later, she was back in the UK, living in London, and writing plays.

Once published, her witty comedies became instantly popular, and were performed on the London stage throughout the 1670s and 1680s. Her most famous play is *The Forced Marriage*, which was first performed in 1670.

Behn is famed for being the first Englishwoman to make her living as a writer, becoming a translator and essayist as well a working on her own literary oevre. Her best-known novel *Oroonoko, The History of the Royal Slave,* was published in 1688. Based on her life in Suriname, the novel tells the story of a European woman who befriends Oroonoko, a prince who was captured in Africa and had been sold as a slave. The book is now considered to be a classic of colonial literature, written with

Behn's first-hand knowledge of the slave trade in Suriname, and life in the colony at that time.

Behn's writings are popular not only because she was a strong, independent woman, who took control of her own destiny, but also because of her depiction of Restoration England and of a life in slavery. She introduced some of our most memorable phrases, such as "Faith, sir, we are here today and gone tomorrow!" (from *A Lucky Mistake*)

She was born in Kent, and will always be remembered as one of our own, but she is buried Westminster Abbey, afforded the full honours that are due to her with a plaque in Poets Corner. No woman before her had won such an accolade. Unfortunately, at the time of her death she was reduced to living in relative poverty.

Her gravestone reads:

'MRS APHRA BEHN DYED APRIL 16 A.D. 1689. Here lies a Proof that Wit can never be Defence enough against Mortality.'

St Augustine's Abbey, Canterbury

7

John Betjeman

(1906-1984)

The poet and writer Sir John Betjeman stayed briefly in Kent in 1929, when he came to Birchington with his employer, Sir Horace Plunkett. They stayed at The Beresford Hotel, which Betjeman described as "furnished in that Japanese style so popular with the wives of Anglo-Indian Colonels . . ." Nevertheless, his employer was paying for his bed and board, so he was quite happy.

This was probably the time visited Westgate-on-Sea and wrote the poem of the same name, drawing heavily on artistic licence, and downplaying the ecclesiastical nature of the bells' true message. Hearing the bells, he reflects on the memories they evoke.

Later, he composed the poem *Margate 1940*, which was a work full of nostalgia for the pre-war period, describing a stay at The Queens Highcliffe Hotel. It was published in the 1945 anthology *New Bats for Old Belfries*, and was actually set in the nearby suburb of Cliftonville. Sadly, the hotel was demolished in the 1970s.

The Queens and The Highcliffe were originally two of three adjacent hotels, with Kimber's Hotel in the middle. They merged into one hotel in 1911. Betjeman contrasts the neatness of the pre-war gardens with the neglected feel of the gardens post-war, remembering good times at the hotel. He ponders on the gaiety of the English seaside holiday, suggesting that such memories gave meaning to soldiers fighting a seemingly pointless war.

High Street, Canterbury

8

Robert Bridges

(1844-1930)

Poet Laureate Robert Seymour Bridges was born in the autumn of 1844 in Upper Walmer, just outside Deal and baptized at the local church in December of that year. His childhood home, Roselands was on the High Street, and his father, Thomas, is listed in the 1851 census as a magistrate. The family had seven servants to help them, and the children were schooled by a Scottish governess.

Having enjoyed an early childhood in rural East Kent, as part of a large and prosperous local family, Bridges was left without a father when he was just nine years old. After an appropriate period of mourning, Mrs Bridges re-married and the family moved to Yorkshire, becoming the second family of an Anglican vicar.

Luckily, money was available for the children's schooling and Bridges was sent to Eton in 1854, from where he went on to study at Oxford and then to St Bartholomew's Hospital in London, where he studied medicine. He struggled with the exams, however, and finally gained his qualification in 1874 in Dublin.

It was clear that medicine was not his first love, and in 1882, at the age of 38, and after less than ten years practising, he retired, partly from increasing trouble with a lung condition, and partly from the desire to devote time to his writing.

Bridges' first book of poetry was published in 1873, and by 1913, he became Britain's Poet Laureate. His work is known for its base in Christian theosophy and for its classical construction, bringing attention to the beauty of the natural world.

He travelled widely in Europe, living for many months in both France and Germany, and the influence of these countries, as well as his first impressions of the landscapes and sea views of East Kent, shine through is work.

He is not buried in Kent, but is mentioned on the Bridges family monument in the parish church at St Nicholas-at-Wade. The poet would have been a frequent visitor, perhaps even meeting once again with his former nurse, who remained working for the family for many years.

9

John Buchan

(1875-1940)

Scottish writer John Norman Stuart Buchan, author of *The 39 Steps,* came to Broadstairs with his family in 1914, despite the recent declaration of war and the very real possibility of an invasion. The couple's daughter Alice was recovering from an operation and sea air had been prescribed by a doctor to aid recovery.

The family lodged at St Ronan's Guesthouse which once stood at 71 Stone Road, near to his wife's cousin, who was renting St Cuby, a villa on North Foreland. The families got on well together, and it soon became obvious that things would be easier if they shared the villa.

The holiday was marred by the fact that Buchan began to suffer serious abdominal pain, and became bedridden by what was later diagnosed as a duodenal ulcer. While he was recovering, he started work on a detective novel as a distraction from the pain. He had already toyed with the idea of writing a thriller, wanting it to be more than just a straightforward story and now he started to develop his ideas in earnest, with fully-developed characters and a detailed conclusion,

St Cuby rested on the top of the cliffs and was joined to the beach by a set of steps set into the chalk. Taking inspiration from his surroundings, the house became Trafalgar Lodge in the novel that was to become *The Thirty-Nine Steps*.

The cliff was high, and the wooden steps zigzagged down through three tunnels and two shafts cut into the chalk; there were 79 shallow steps in total. Shrouded from view at the top and inaccessible at high tide at the lower end, the steps, possibly cut by smugglers, created a perfect setting for espionage.

Time and weather have taken their toll on the old wooden steps, and even the concrete ones which replaced them have now started to crumble. The public are denied access to the shaft, but if you stand at the bottom when the area is deserted, with the waves breaking on the shore behind you, it is not hard to see it as the setting of thrills and skulduggery.

Despite the family's need to stay near the villa for the sake of the invalids, they visited Broadstairs often enough for it to appear in the novel as the town of Bradgate. Other places are also recognisable: The Royal Albion Hotel becomes The Griffin Hotel and the North Goodwin Lightship becomes the ship on Cock Sands.

The Ruff, described by Buchan from the beach, is clearly the North Foreland cliff.

> '. . . I had a view of the line of turf along the clifftop, with seats placed at intervals, and the little square plots, railed in and planted with bushes, whence the staircases descended to the beach'.

The sight of a 'young man on a bicycle, with a bag of golf-clubs slung on his back' would not be unusual even today, as the North Foreland Golf Club is nearby.

After the holiday, the Buchan family returned to London, and more rest was prescribed for the ailing writer. Although he worked as a war correspondent for The Times, he continued to write fiction in his spare time. *The Thirty-Nine Steps* was finished in 1915 and serialised in Blackwood's Magazine before being published as a hardcover book in the autumn.

The story of John Buchan and *The Thirty-Nine Steps* is nicely rounded off when we learn that a local carpenter was given some of the wood from the dismantled steps and used it to make three sets of bookends. One pair was given to the owners of St Cuby, one to Alfred Hitchcock and one to Buchan himself. Each set has an inscription giving its provenance

10

Elizabeth Carter

(1717-1806)

Elizabeth Carter is best known for her translation work, but she had a wide academic repertoire and was much-respected. The red brick house she owned in Deal is still very much as it was when she lived there, although the town itself has now changed beyong all recognition. From being a port of great significance for sailing ships, the town went through a period of depression, before reinventing itself as an artists' retreat full of historical detail.

Carter was the eldest daughter of Dr Nicholas Carter, who held a post as perpetual curate at St George's Church in the centre of the town. The church is just a short walk down Middle Street and along the High Street from the Carter house. She was baptized, however, at St Leonards Church on the London Road.

Dr Carter took responsibility for his daughter's education, and tutored her in Greek, Latin and Hebrew. Seeing her aptitude for languages, he sent her to board for a year with a refugee minister in Canterbury, during which time she became fluent in French. She later continued her studies in language, and learnt Italian, Spanish, Arabic, Portuguese and German. She pushed herself hard, and often resorted to taking snuff in order to keep awake while she studied. This habit stayed with her to the end of her life.

By the time she was twenty her father encouraged Carter to visit widely in London, and to spend a portion of her year in the town, where she became well-known and adopted the title 'Mrs' although she never married.

The first of Carter's published works were submitted to The Gentleman's Magazine when she was only sixteen. The editor happened to be a friend of her father, and in their group was the eminent Dr Samuel Johnson, with whom Carter formed a friendship. Later, she was to edit some editions of *The Rambler*, a twice-weekly periodical largely written by Johnson.

Johnson considered the writer to be a personal friend, and remarked that "My old friend Mrs. Carter could make a pudding as well as translate Epictetus from the Greek and work a handkerchief as well as compose a poem." drawing attention to the fact that she was not removed from the more traditional female roles of the time, despite her academic accomplishments.

Soon after this, she embarked on a translation of *All the Works of Epictetus Which are Now Extant*, for which she is still remembered. The work was not published until 1758, ten years after it was started. This, however, was the first English translation of Epictetus and Elizabeth earned a profit of £1,000 which would be worth in excess of £180,000 today.

Carter used the money, along with an inheritance from her uncle, to buy the house in South Street that is now known as Elizabeth Carter House, where she lived with her father from 1762.

By this time, Carter was a recognised academic and a member of the Bluestocking Circle, translating poems from French and Italian into English. She was considered to be one of the most learned of all the members, and is still thought of as one of the more learned Englishwomen of her time.

Nicholas Carter died in 1774, when his daughter was 57, and she inherited a modest sum. She was also lucky enough to receive an annuity of £100 pa from one of her old friends, Elizabeth Montagu. This started a trend, and two other friends also left her money, giving her the income she needed to continue her independent lifestyle.

Carter kept the house in Deal, splitting her time between there and London. She died in London at the age of 89 and her memoirs were published a year later. Over the next decade, her letters also made their way into print, showing the continuing public interest in her as a role model and commentator on matters of national interest. Elizabeth Gaskell admired her life, as did Virginia Woolfe, who particularly admired her drive and determination.

11

Geoffrey Chaucer

(1343-1400)

The name Geoffrey Chaucer, Justice of the Peace, MP and finally writer, will be forever linked with Canterbury, because his major work is entitled *The Canterbury Tales*. The journey described in the poem, however, travels through many different places in Kent and because Chaucer died before completing the work, the town of Canterbury is not actually described.

Very little can be verified about the life of Geoffrey Chaucer, even though he held some major public offices, but much can be speculated.

At 14, he became a page to the King Edward III's son Lionel, and in 1359, aged just 16, and went with the King to fight in The Hundred Years War. He was captured, but the £16 ransom was paid by the King. In return, Chaucer joined the diplomatic service.

Chaucer entered into the King's service in 1365, and a year later, married Philippa Roet, a lady-in-waiting to the Queen. During the next ten years, he continued his diplomatic work, and is also known to have entertained the court with his songs and stories.

In 1375 he was given custody of land previously belonging to Edmond Staplegate of Kent, who had obviously fallen from royal favour. He was also received rent from five parcels of land near Sole Court Farm, Nonington while the owner was not yet of the age of majority.

In 1385, aged 42, Chaucer became Justice of the Peace for Kent, sitting four times a year to hear cases, although he may well have lived in London at the time. He held the post for four years, during which time he became Member of Parliament for Kent, giving up his post as Collector of Customs. This was an excellent move, as MPs had voted themselves generous expenses, including travel expenses, which Chaucer was quick to claim.

In 1389 he became Clerk of the King's Work, and it was during this time that he started to write in earnest.

He had already begun several of his major works which were still in embryo form at this time. *The Parliament of Fowls* and *Troilus and Criseyde* were both drafted by the time he went into semi-retirement and he looked more closely at his plans for *The*

Canterbury Tales, a long poem in a style not seen before in English literature.

The 17,000 line poem tells twenty-four stories narrated by the individuals who travel together from London to Canterbury to visit the shrine of Thomas Becket. The stories were told as part of a competition, with the prize of a meal at The Tabard Inn, Southwark, on their return. The journey would probably have taken four days, with stops at Dartford, Rochester and Ospringe, so a way of passing the time would have been welcome. The pilgrims left London, passing through Greenwich 'with many a blackguard in it', and travelled down the Darent Valley past Eynsford, Rochester, Aylesford, Charing and Eastwell, eventually passing through Boughton Aluph.

Greenwich, Deptford and Rochester are all mentioned in passing, and Boughton-under-Blean has a slightly longer reference in The Canon's Yeoman's Tale.

> " Whan that tolde was the lif of Seinte Cecile,
> Br we had ridden fully five mile,
> At Boughton under blee us gan atake
> A man, that clothed was in clothes blake,
> And undernethe he wered a white surplis."

The pilgrims enter Canterbury via Harbledown, which Chaucer calls 'Bob-up-and-Down'.

> 'Bobbe-up-and-doun,
> Under the Blee,
> in Canterbury Weye.'

The pilgrim's tales are represented in the Canterbury Visitor attraction *The Canterbury Tales*, and although the cathedral would now be unrecognisable to the medieval pilgrims, it is still a fascinating place to experience Canterbury as it might have been in medieval times.

In 1399, we know that Chaucer moved back to London, but it is unclear where he was in the interim. It is assumed that he lived in Kent during this time, possibly with his sister Kate Manning in Greenwich.

In 1400 the retelling of the stories in *The Canterbury Tales* came to an abrupt end when Chaucer died, although the exact date is unknown. Scholars generally agree on the date of circa 1400 and that he was then buried in Westminster Abbey.

Rochester Castle

12

Richard Church

(1893-1972)

Poet and novelist Richard Thomas Church was born in Battersea, but lived most of his life in Kent. He came to love the Kent countryside and published an anthology of poems about the county.

Church and his second wife Katherina moved to The Oasthouse, Curtisden Green, near Goudhurst in 1939, which the couple renovated.

Following her death in 1965, he moved into The Old Stable at Scotney Castle, Goudhurst, and two years later he married again and the couple moved to The Priest's House at Sissinghurst Castle, near Cranbrook where Church lived until his death.

Church's love for Kent is reflected in his poetry and in 1964 he published an anthology of works on the county called *The Little Kingdom: A Kentish Collection,* which presents an idealised version of the rural idyll he craved. He also wrote non-fiction, bringing to press *A History of Kent*, which includes autobiographical notes, such as details of his time in the Home Guard during WW2. Published in 1948, it includes descriptions of the countryside and the emotions it engendered in the writer, as well as a history of the county.

13

Winston Churchill

(1874-1965)

Winston Leonard Spencer-Churchill was born in Oxfordshire, but spent over 40 years living at Chartwell, two miles south of Westerham and less than ten miles from Sevenoaks. While at the house, he wrote several of his most important works, including *The World Crisis, Marlborough* and *The History of the English Speaking Peoples.* In 1953 he was awarded the Nobel Prize for Literature for his contribution to the written and spoken word. The official wording says that the prize had was awarded for 'his mastery of historical and biographical description as well as for brilliant oratory in defending exalted human values'.

Churchill wrote for work as well as for pleasure, and 135 of his speeches have been published.

His most important work was *A History of the English-Speaking Peoples*, which appeared in four volumes (1956–58). Although *Savrola* (1900) was Churchill's only novel, he also wrote several short stories.

When they first bought Chartwell in the early 1920s, the Churchill family used the property solely as a weekend retreat only moving in permanently ten years later. While the renovations were in progress, the family rented a farmhouse in Westerham to be close enough to supervise the work. As well as fixing structural problems, such as damp, the contractors landscaped the gardens. Eventually, three guest cottages were built in the grounds and a large swimming pool was added. The lakes and Lady Churchill's rose garden were later enhancements.

By 1938 the house had five reception rooms, nineteen bedrooms (with dressing rooms), eight bathrooms, and eighty acres of gardens and parkland. The house, the garden and the Kentish landscape all offered a refuge from the stress of Churchill's life as a politician, and this is reflected in his many landscape paintings. He loved the house and is often quoted as saying "A day away from Chartwell is a day wasted."

In the 1940s, the couple bought Chartwell Farm, Parkside Farm, and Bardogs Farm, but they did not prove profitable, and Churchill turned his attention to breeding racehorses, which he did with some success.

During the Second World War, Churchill frequently had business in Dover, both to review first-hand the damage from

German bombs and also to attend meetings in the war tunnels built into the cliffs under Dover Castle.

In 1941, Churchill was appointed Lord Warden and Admiral of the Cinque Ports, an honour which came with an official residence (Walmer Castle) and an official uniform. He never made Walmer Castle his home, but he did often wear the uniform. He also flew the official flag of The Lord Warden at Chartwell.

By 1945, Chartwell required such expensive upkeep that it was beyond the Churchill's means. A group of friends banded together to fund the purchase on behalf of The National Trust, on the understanding that the family could continue to occupy the property at a nominal rent.

The house is still owned and maintained by The National Trust, and visitors can see a wealth of personal memorabilia, including Churchill's study and library and the Mary Cot playhouse which he built for his daughter. His art studio is a separate building, and is hung with some of his landscape paintings. There are two statues of Churchill nearby, one on Westerham Green, and one of him and Clementine in the gardens at Chartwell.

Churchill was elected an Honorary Life Member of the Association of Men of Kent and Kentish Men in 1949. In 1953 he suffered a stroke and retired to Chartwell to recover. He returned to London for two more years before he retired permanently to Chartwell in 1955.

14

S T Coleridge

(1772-1834)

Samuel Taylor Coleridge was one of the founders of the Romantic Movement in England. His poems *Kubla Khan* and *The Rime of the Ancient Mariner* are some of the most quoted works in English literature.

Coleridge was a regular visitor to Ramsgate during the 1820s and 1830s, during the reign of King George IV who loved Kent and had given Ramsgate the title Royal Harbour of Ramsgate in 1821, having been impressed by the friendliness of the town

Princess Victoria, later to be Queen Victoria, also holidayed in Ramsgate as a child, and this added to the town's popularity. A tourist trade developed, and it became a very fashionable destination.

The quickest way to get from London to Ramsgate in the 1820s was by steamship, and Coleridge availed himself of this new mode of transport, enjoying the novelty of the experience and the thrill of the engines.

He visited Ramsgate ten times in the decade up to 1833 and lodged at several of the houses in Wellington Crescent, Ramsgate, which had been recently built and named after The Duke of Wellington in honour of his successes in The Napoleonic Wars. With their intricate wrought-iron railings and pagoda-style canopied balconies, these properties were at the height of modern style. A blue plaque has been placed outside Number 3 to recognise the poet's connection to the house, but he also variously stayed at numbers 7, 28 and 29 and other lodgings in Ramsgate.

The Delinquent Travellers, written in 1821, contains, amongst the poesy, a tiny glimpse of the Kent coast as travellers prepare to cross The English Channel.

> 'But ere we cross the main once more,
> Methinks, along my native shore,
> Dismounting from my steed I'll stray
> Beneath the cliffs of Dumpton Bay,
> Where, Ramsgate and Broadstairs between,
> Rude caves and grated doors are seen:'

Sadly, the next passages describe how he is captured by smugglers and tossed into a waiting ship, to be carried off to new lands, but the details of the Kent coast show a real local knowledge.

Coleridge preferred to come to Kent in the autumn, when the crowds of holidaymakers had dispersed and the landladies had dropped their prices. Surprisingly, the rents for a house in Wellington Crescent were higher than that for a similar house in London, so the fact that he came at all gives credit to the place – it certainly wasn't for the economy of living, although he did benefit from the generosity of his friends in finding somewhere the stay, often joining them at their own holiday let.

He loved the town, and stayed for 6-8 weeks on each occasion, hoping that the fresh air and sea-bathing opportunities would improve his health.

The sea-bathing was accomplished by means of the newly-introduced bathing machines that could be hired on the beach. He describes the experience in 1821 in a letter to a friend.

> 'I was myself very unwell on Monday & Yesterday – but this morning, I have cleared up again, and had such a Trio of Plunges into the very heart, Liver, and Lights of three towering Billows this morning, the last of which fairly hurried me back, I might almost say, into the Machine – but actually, to the top-most step of the Ladder ... The wave set the Carpet afloat, and had I not instantly called out to Philpott, that his Pot was over-full, I should have had my ... Cloathes, seized by the grim old Surgeon without any to redress me... It was glorious! I watched each time from the top-step for a high Wave coming, and then with my utmost power of projection shot myself off into it, for all the world like a Congreve Rocket into a Whale.'

Another 'cure' he found soothing was the salt-water shower:

> 'I have certainly been much benefited, in praesenti, by the warm salt Shower Baths – standing with my legs in a Tub at the temperature of near a 100, & receiving from 30 to 40 gallons of salt water of from 90 to 100 [Fahrenheit]'

By 1822 scandal was beginning to grow around Samuel's continued friendship with the wife of his friend Gillman. The couple often met in Ramsgate without Gillman, and tongues wagged. He remained friends with both Ann Gillham and her husband, so perhaps the rumours were just that – rumours.

Although he supposedly came to Ramsgate to write, Coleridge and his friends spent a lot of time socializing and attending local events. He took a keen interest in everything around him, and too a tour of the new Synagogue in Ramsgate, erected by Sir Moses Montefiore in 1833, as well as Canterbury Cathedral, some twenty miles distant.

On his last holiday in Ramsgate in 1833, the writer met with his old friend William Wordsworth, who was staying in nearby Broadstairs. Once again, Coleridge was staying with his friends the Gillmans at Bellvue Place on East Cliff, and mentions as meeting with the daughter of Sir Walter Scott. He called her a "truly an interesting and love-compelling woman".

Coleridge always intended to return to the town with his family, but unfortunately, he died before he could do so. He died in 1834, and his friend Gillman followed him five years later. Ann Gillman moved to Ramsgate and lived for another twenty years. During her last years, she was almost blind, and liked her granddaughter to read passages from the work of Coleridge.

The girl recalls that the old lady would sometimes sigh "If only..." during the readings, "Ah, my dear, if only..."

Canterbury Cathedral

15

Wilkie Collins

(1824-1889)

As was often the custom in the 19th century, William Wilkie Collins was named after his father and his godfather. To distinguish him from his father, he adopted his middle name for general use. Collins first came to Kent as a child in 1833 and it became a much-loved holiday destination. He stayed in Dover on several occasions, but was particularly fond of Ramsgate and Broadstairs. While in Kent, he developed his writing and is widely recognised as the writer of the first detective novel, *The Moonstone*

In 1852, Collins lodged at 10 Camden Crescent in Dover alongside Charles Dickens, who had also taken rooms with his family. The pair had first met in 1851 and struck up an immediate friendship. Collins was one of the first visitors to Dickens' house at Gads Hill, Higham, when he bought it in 1857. Collins loved the location of the lodging house, overlooking the harbour, saying that "The sea air acts on me as if it was all distilled from laudanum." During the stay, he walked to Canterbury to see the cathedral, and marvelled at the sight of the building "white and brilliant against the bluest of skies". The towns are between 15 and 20 miles apart, depending on which route you take so, not unsurprisingly, he took a carriage for the journey back to Dover.

In 1853 Collins once again holidayed in Kent with Charles Dickens, this time staying with Dickens and his family at 3 Albion Villas, Folkestone. Set high on the cliffs, the view is now partially obscured by trees, but Collins and the Dickens family would have had a view far out over The English Channel.

Ramsgate, in particular, was a favourite destination for Collins, and he stayed several times at 14 Nelson Crescent during the 1860s and 1870s. He also lived at 27 Wellington Crescent at the same time! At Number 14 he lived with his housekeeper Caroline Graves and her daughter, and at Number 27 he registered as Mr & Mrs Dawson and stayed there with his lover Martha Rudd and their children. Another Ramsgate day-tripper was Charles Dickens and the two often met while in town.

During the 1870s Collins was so frequent a visitor to Ramsgate that he joined the yacht club and the town became the setting for scenes in novels including *Poor Miss Finch* (1872) and *The Law and the Lady* (1875). In *The Fallen Leaves* (1879) he describes Ramsgate, talking about "...the cries of the children at play, the shouts of the donkey boys driving their poor beasts, the distant notes of brass instruments playing a waltz, and the mellow music of small waves breaking on the sand".

Collins also enjoyed Broadstairs, sailing from there to Dunkirk in the summer of 1858, and he used it as a retreat for writing. Collins and Dickens stayed at The Royal Albion Hotel, Broadstairs, in 1859, while Dickens was working on his novel *Nicholas Nickleby.*

Collins later rented Church Hill Cottage, on the Ramsgate Road in Broadstairs for six weeks and tasked himself with writing *The Woman in White*, working from 10am until 3pm in the afternoon. Although he was ill and suffering from a want of funds at the time, he appreciated the location of the cottage, with gardens and fields behind, and nothing between it and the sea but open downs with "a fresh breeze flowing in from the sea all day long" at the front. It has been said that the title of the book, which initially eluded him, was inspired by the lighthouse at Ramsgate, which seemed to Collins as white and tall as a lonely woman. Dickens was staying nearby and they dined alternately at one another's lodgings.

Collins returned to Broadstairs 1861, and the next year was fortunate enough to rent Fort House, immortalised by Charles Dickens as Bleak House, while *No Name* was serialised.

The two writers remained friends and literary soul mates until Dickens' sudden death in 1870. Such was their close working relationship that Collins was asked to complete *Edwin Drood,* which Dickens had left unfinished. He politely refused.

16

Joseph Conrad

(1857-1924)

Josef Korzeniowski, best known for his novels *Lord Jim* and *Heart of Darkness* was born in Ukraine, but due to moving political borders, was deemed at the time to be Polish. In 1886, aged 29, he assumed British citizenship, anglicising his first name to Joseph, and using his middle name (Konrad) as a surname.

He was almost 40 when he married and settled in Pent Farm, Postling, situated on the Kent Downs five miles north of Hythe, which was rented to him by his friend Ford Madox Ford. He lived there from 1898 until 1906, when the friends had an argument about the payment of the rent and he felt that he had to leave, but it was here that he wrote both novels and short stories, including *Lord Jim, Heart of Darkness,* and *The Secret Agent.*

His next move was to Church Hill Cottage in Aldington, north-west of Hythe, in 1909. He found the cottage 'dark, damp and cold' and future owners must have agreed with him, as they knocked three cottages into one to create the current house. He then rented Capel House in Orlestone, five miles south of Ashford, from 1910-1919 where he wrote *A Smile of Fortune* and the novels *Chance* and *Victory*.

The family were happy in Orlestone and made many friends in the area. Sadly the owner eventually decided that he wanted to live in the house himself and the Conrad family moved briefly to Wye, living at Spring Grove, Harville Road (now a school) and eventually settled in Bishopsbourne, south of Canterbury, where they lived in a large Georgian house called Oswalds from 1920 until the writer's death in 1924.

Conrad died in Bishopsbourne and is buried in Canterbury Cemetery. His tomb is registered as a listed building.

17

Noel Coward

(1899-1973)

London-born Noel Peirce Coward, successful in so many of the creative and performing arts, first got to know and love the Kentish countryside in the early 1920, when he and a friend stayed in a cottage at Dymchurch for several weeks. One of the objectives of the trip was to find an affordable cottage that Coward could rent while he continued his writing. He found a little cottage in St Mary-in-the-Marsh, next door to The Star Inn and, as was often the case with village inns, opposite the church. It was to the churchyard that Coward often retreated, to sit in the quietness and write.

Coward bought his first house in Kent in 1926. He purchased Goldenhurst Farm, in Giggers Green Road, Aldington. The village lies twelve miles outside Ashford, just on the edge of the Romney Marsh and is now designated as an Area of Outstanding Natural Beauty. It has a rich history, including being the home of the infamous Aldington Gang of smugglers, who operated from The Walnut Tree pub a century earlier.

The writer updated and extended the farmhouse, linking several of the farm buildings together to make one large house, which, interestingly, has subsequently been divided into two dwellings, Goldenhurst and The Old House. The building is of traditional construction, having a timber frame clad with Kentish ragstone and part-hung with tiles. The property also had a large garden and Coward employed five gardeners to keep it under control. One of his most famous works, *Cavalcade*, was written at the farm.

In 1945, Goldenhurst was requisitioned by The War Office and Coward bought Kay's Bluff, a property at St Margaret's Bay on the far eastern coast of the county which he renamed White Cliffs. Once again, he put his own stamp on the house, updating the heating and lighting and redecorating throughout. At the time, there were four houses in the location, at the bottom of the cliffs, with their toes dipping into the English Channel, and Coward was frustrated by the lack of the isolation he needed to continue his work. Unable to buy the other houses, due to wartime restrictions, his friends and family bought them, so he could remain secluded.

It was here that he wrote *Blithe Spirit* and *Still Life*, the play which became the heart-breaking *Brief Encounter*. In 1951, he sold the house to Ian Fleming. The two had met in Jamaica, and he and Fleming already owned property near each other, so their friendship continued.

Life was not all work, however, and he hosted parties for his friends. Graham Payn, Joseph Cotton, Gertrude Lawrence, John Mills, Spencer Tracey, Katherine Hepburn and Daphne du Maurier are all said to have been entertained at the tiny cottage, enjoying (or not) the stiff breezes that blew in off the sea. He also encouraged his friends to use the house when he was not in residence.

When he was not working, his lifestyle was less reclusive, and he travelled extensively both across The Channel and around the local area, going to the cinema and even attending 'am dram' productions at Deal. He also travelled to London, often more than once a week, to see friends and attend the theatre.

Despite all the work he did on the house, including a mammoth project to shore up the chalk cliffs which reared behind it, he moved back to Aldington when the war ended and kept Goldenhurst Farm until 1956.

18

Charles Darwin

(1809-1882)

The scientist Charles Robert Darwin was born in Shrewsbury, but spent the last forty years of his life in Kent. It was while he was living here that he formulated and published his iconic work *On The Origin of Species.*

Darwin was 33 when he and his wife Emma moved to Downe House, Cudham Road, in the village of Down in 1842, with the first three of their ten children. The village is now part of Greater London, but until 1965 was firmly within the county of Kent.

The couple chose the house because of the 18 acres of land that came with it, meaning that the neighbours were neither "too near nor too far. The couple were "pleased with the diversified appearance of the vegetation proper to a chalk district ... and still more pleased with the extreme quietness and rusticity of the place".

To further seclude the growing family, the lane that ran along the front of the house was lowered, so the house was shielded from the prying eyes of passers-by. Darwin was so protective of his privacy that he even had a mirror mounted outside his study so he could see anyone approaching.

As the family grew, Darwin extended the house, adding an extra wing in 1846 and a small two-story extension in 1858. Another significant improvement was the creation of an experimental section of the kitchen garden. The work Darwin carried out here formed the basis for his work *Different Forms of Flowers on Plants of the Same Species*, published in 1877.

In 1850, the family, now including seven children, travelled to Ramsgate for a holiday, staying at 8 Paragon, overlooking the newly-completed Royal Harbour. The reason for the visit was to improve their daughter Anne's health. Unfortunately, the child became worse and the family had to return home within weeks and Anne died the following year.

Further tragedy struck the Darwin family in 1858, when an outbreak of scarlet fever hit Down village and their son Charles died.

From 1855 until 1867 Darwin kept a notebook to record the results of his experiments in the garden and greenhouse and from the 1860s onwards, his work with plants intensified. He built a hothouse where he could pursue his botanic investigations, and which allowed him to grow more exotic plants than were available locally. The work in this hothouse led to *On the Various Contrivances by which British and Foreign Orchids are Fertilised by Insects* (1862).

The Sandwalk is a pretty feature of the property, created by the Darwins soon after they moved in. It is edged with native trees and was used daily by Darwin for meditation; he called it his 'thinking path'.

On the 1881 census, Darwin is recorded still living in Downe with his wife, five children, grandson, niece, cousin and a friend from Germany. The family have eight servants.

After Darwin's death in 1882 the house was kept empty for some time, then sold, to The Downe House School for girls which remained there for the forty years. In 1996 the property was acquired by English Heritage, and visitors can now see the house, the grounds and the lovingly restored recreation of Darwin's study plus a replica of his cabin on HMS Beagle.

19

Daniel Defoe

(1660-1731)

Produced at the beginning of the 18th century, one of Daniel Defoe's best known works is his *A Tour Through the Whole Isle of Gre*at Britain. Published in three volumes between 1724-1726, he describes and critiques the towns and villages he visits, not all of them in very flattering terms. He describes Sandwich, for instance as "an old decayed port, miserable town"

Nor did he think much of Dover "Neither Dover nor its castle has any thing of note to be said of them, but what is in common with their neighbours; the castle is old, useless, decay'd, and serves for little; but to give the title and honour of government to men of quality, with a salary, and sometimes to those that want one."

He also had some scathing criticism of Tunbridge Wells:

> "In a word, Tunbridge wants nothing that can add to the felicities of life, or that can make a man or woman compleatly happy, always provided they have money; for without money a man is no-body at Tunbridge,'

He did, however, like Maidstone, noting "Maidstone is eminent for the plenty of provisions, and richness of lands in the country all round it, and for the best market in the county, not Rochester, no not Canterbury excepted."

He may not have rated the market at Canterbury highly, but he recognised the history it contained: "The latter was a town which for which its antiquity seems to be its greatest beauty. The houses are truly ancient, and the many ruins of churches, chapels, oratories, and smaller cells of religious people, making the place look like a general ruin a little recovered."

Defoe's most intriguing link with the county of Kent is explained by Wallace Harvey in his 1989 book, *Seasalter and the Mystery of Robinson Crusoe*. The book provides compelling evidence that Daniel Defoe was very familiar with that part of the north coast of Kent near Seasalter and Whitstable, suggesting that he may even have had relatives in the area. Drawing on the knowledge that Defoe regularly used real places as a basis for his writing, Harvey has meticulously researched the coastline from the 16th century and suggests that Robinson Crusoe was actually shipwrecked on the Columbine sandbank and came ashore at Seasalter. Details such as the post on which Crusoe carved notches, the description of an offshore wreck used as accommodation by seasonal workers, and that, before the building of the sea wall, parts of Whitstable were once an island at high tide, seem to support his theory.

We may never have this confirmed by hard evidence, but the details provided by Harvey seem, to me, to make the fact indisputable.

Toll Gate, Sandwich

20

Charles Dickens

(1812-1870)

One of England's best loved and most widely recognised authors, Charles John Huffam Dickens' time in Kent can be separated into two main locations, although of course he visited numerous places across the county at many different times. Broadstairs and Rochester both hold an annual Dickens Festival, claiming him as their own.

Dickens' father was a Navy Pay Office clerk, and was posted to Chatham when Dickens was five years old. After a brief stay in Sheerness, on the Isle of Sheppey, the family moved to Number 2 Ordnance Terrace, Chatham (now renumbered No.11) and stayed there until 1821 when they moved to 18 St Mary's Place, The Brook, which was closer to the dockyard. The property can be seen from the outside, but is now a private residence. However, his time there made a lasting impression on Dickens.

While he was young, father and son took long walks together, out into the surrounding countryside, and it was on one of these walks that the pair spotted Gads Hill Place, Crutches Lane, Higham, just under five miles from Chatham Dockyard. Quite a long walk for little legs! Dickens thought the house was "the most beautiful house ever seen" and they joked about one day owning such a fine house.

"My poor father used to bring me to look at it, and used to say that if ever I grew up to be a clever man perhaps I might own that house, or another such house," Dickens recalled in 1857.

This north-west corner of the county is where Dickens lived for most of his life. He honeymooned with his wife Catherine in Chalk, three miles east of Gravesend, in 1836, staying in Craddock's Cottage, which has now been renamed Lesley's Cottage. Nearby, the forge on Lower Higham Road is said to be the place that inspired Joe Gargery's workshop in *The Mystery of Edwin Drood*.

Dickens did eventually buy a house as nice as Gads Hill Place – Gad's Hill Place itself! After living in several place in London, he finally moved to Kent in 1860. The house has undergone many changes in its lifetime and is now a school. In fact, it featured as a school in *The Ghost of Christmas Past*, being very recognisably "a mansion of dull red brick with a little weathercock-surmounted cupola on the roof and a bell hanging in it".

The family made many alterations to the house, including the addition of a Swiss Chalet in the garden which was reached by a tunnel underneath the road which bisected the property. He used the Swiss Cottage as a study, and it was here that he wrote *Great Expectations, The Uncommercial Traveller, Our Mutual Friend* and *The Mystery of Edwin Drood.*

The last was never finished, and avid fans like to read and speculate on what the ending might have been. It is set in and around Rochester, in the guise of the town Cloisterham, and is described with affection: "Its antiquities and ruins are surpassingly beautiful, with a lusty ivy gleaming in the sun, and the rich trees waving in the balmy air. Changes of glorious light from moving boughs, songs of birds, scents from gardens, woods, and fields - or, rather, from the one great garden of the whole cultivated island in its yielding time - penetrate into the Cathedral, subdue its earthy odour, and preach the Resurrection and the Life. The cold stone tombs of centuries ago grow warm; and flecks of brightness dart into the sternest marble corners of the building, fluttering there like wings."

When he needed a break, Dickens would take long walks in the Kent countryside or drop into the local pub, the Sir John Falstaff. It is said that the obliging landlord would send beer to Gads Hill Place when Dickens was too immersed in his writing to leave the study.

When staying in Folkestone in 1855, he wrote about his walks, and how his narratives consumed him, even when outside "how I roll down hills and climb up cliffs; how the new story is everywhere, heaving on the sea, flying with the clouds, blowing in the wind; how I settle to nothing."

Mr Augustus Snodgrass describes Rochester in *The Pickwick Papers*, reflecting what we can only assume was Dickens own opinion of the town, starting with Rochester castle

> "Ah! fine place, ... glorious pile--frowning walls--tottering arches--dark nooks--crumbling staircases--old cathedral too--earthy smell--pilgrims' feet wore away the old steps--little Saxon doors--confessionals like money-takers' boxes at theatres--queer customers those monks--popes, and lord treasurers, and all sorts of old fellows, with great red faces, and broken noses, turning up every day--buff jerkins too--match-locks--sarcophagus--fine place--old legends too--strange stories: capital."

So many places in the town are associated with Dickens, from his own life and the life of his characters, that it would be futile to try to list them all here. I would urge you to find one of the excellent Town Trails available and tread the streets as Dickens did – so much is still as he would have known it.

Look out for The Six Poor Travellers House which was used in *The Seven Poor Travellers* stories. Restoration House which was the inspiration for Miss Haversham's Satis House, and many other buildings which are mentioned in passing, from The Guildhall where Pip was apprenticed in *Great Expectations* to The Corn Exchange Clock and Eastgate House.

Charles Dickens first went to Broadstairs in 1837, aged 25, and returned frequently for the next two decades. As with Rochester, he stayed at and commented upon so many places, that there is only room to mention a few.

In 1839, the family stayed briefly in The High Street before taking rooms for a month at 40 Albion Street, which is now

Number 12 and forms part of The Albion Hotel, overlooking Viking Bay. It was here that he wrote part of *The Pickwick Papers* and also worked on the novel that was to become *Nicholas Nickleby*.

It was from his rooms at the hotel that he saw Mary Pearson Strong becoming irate at the number of donkeys that passed her home. The two became friends, and Dickens used her as the basis for the character of Betsey Trotwood in the novel David Copperfield, and her home "a neat little cottage with cheerful bow window" now houses the Dickens House Museum.

Dickens loved the little seaside town of Broadstairs, writing about it as 'Our Watering Place' in 1852 in Household Words, a weekly journal, and he returned each summer for the next twelve years. He wrote "You cannot think how delightful and fresh the place is and how good the walks." In a letter to a friend, and, later, 'It is more delightful here than I can express. Corn growing, larks singing, garden full of flowers, Fresh air on the sea – O it is wonderful!'

In 1851 the Dickens family moved into Fort House while their house in London was being refurbished, and this is where he started to write *Bleak House*, the novel after which the house is now named. He based much of the description of the house on Fort House, but as avid fans will know, used artistic licence to relocate the house to St Albans.

> "It is a favourite home of mine perched by itself on top of the cliff with the green corn growing all about it and the larks singing invisible all day long...the freshness of the sea and the associations of the place – I finished David Copperfield in this same airy nest – have set me to work with great vigour."

The building has been greatly enlarged since he lived in it, by the addition of a west wing; when he was there is consisted only of the rooms within the main, square building.

Dickens loved the contrast of the rolling countryside to the quaint fishing-town of Broadstairs. He travelled by paddle-steamer to the town, changing at Ramsgate, and sometimes staying overnight in The Royal Oak Hotel. Once there, he could often be found in The Tartar Frigate, Harbour Street, which he described as “the cosiest little sailors’ inn that is to be met around the coast.”. One of his earliest works in *Sketches by Boz* was ‘The Tugges of Ramsgate’, a short, comical tale of a family on holiday who take a trip to Ramsgate and stay at The Pegwell Bay Hotel.

He made the most of his time in East Kent, enjoying the surrounding countryside on his daily walks. When Hans Christian Anderson stayed in Ramsgate, he noted that his friend Dickens walked from Broadstairs to say goodbye before his departure. Dickens also walked regularly to Dover, a distance of about 20 miles, and liked to walk up to ten miles after dinner.

Wilkie Collins was another friend who visited regularly, and Dickens’ daughter later married Collins' son in Higham Church.

Another place that Dickens stayed was Lawn House, which has been renamed Archway House. It sits on Fort Road, and it is here that he wrote part of *Barnaby Rudge*, which was first published in 1840, and part of *The Old Curiosity Shop.* He managed to balance work and pleasure, writing: "I am hideously lazy--always bathing, lying in the sun, or walking about. I write a No." (edition of *Barnaby Rudge*) "when the time comes, and dream about it beforehand on cliffs and sands--but as to getting in advance!"

In 1841 Dickens writes to John Forster about being 'unable to resist the brilliancy out of doors' so that he 'breaketh off, rusheth to the machines and plungeth into the sea.'

Dickens described Broadstairs as "one of the freshest and freest little places in the world". In 1843 he wrote to a friend: "This is a little fishing-place; intensely quiet; built on a cliff, whereon—in the centre of a tiny semicircular bay—our house stands; the sea rolling and dashing under the windows. Seven miles out are the Goodwin Sands (you've heard of the Goodwin Sands?) whence floating lights perpetually wink after dark, as if they were carrying on intrigues with the servants. Also there is a big lighthouse called the North Foreland on a hill behind the village, a severe parsonic light, which reproves the young and giddy floaters, and stares grimly out upon the sea. Under the cliff are rare good sands, where all the children assemble every morning and throw up impossible fortifications, which the sea throws down again at high water. Old gentlemen and ancient ladies flirt after their own manner in two reading-rooms and on a great many scattered seats in the open air. Other old gentlemen look all day through telescopes and never see anything. In a bay-window in a one-pair sits, from nine o'clock to one, a gentleman with rather long hair and no neckcloth, who writes and grins as if he thought he were very funny indeed. His name is Boz. At one he disappears, and presently emerges from a bathing-machine, and may be seen—a kind of salmon-coloured porpoise—splashing about in the ocean. After that he may be seen in another bay-window on the ground-floor, eating a strong lunch; after that, walking a dozen miles or so, or lying on his back in the sand reading a book. Nobody bothers him unless they know he is disposed to be talked to; and I am told he is very comfortable indeed. He's as brown as a berry, and they *do* say is a small fortune to the innkeeper who sells beer and cold punch. But this is mere rumour."

In 1851 Dickens characterised Broadstairs in a letter to Lord Carlisle: "The general character of Broadstairs as to size and accommodation was happily expressed by Miss Eden ... saying how grateful she felt to a certain sailor, who asked leave to see her garden, for not plucking it bodily up, and sticking it in his button-hole."

In July 1851, he wrote to his friend Mr Knight, exhorting him to come to Kent: "We will make expeditions to Herne Bay, Canterbury, where not? and drink deep draughts of fresh air. Come! They are beginning to cut the corn. You will never see the country so pretty."

Dickens frequently travelled through Folkestone on his way to visit his sons who were in boarding school in Boulogne, arriving in the town by train and then continuing by steam ship to the continent.

In 1853, he took lodgings in Folkestone while writing *A Child's History of England* and, the essay 'Out of Town', which features Pavilionstone, a town very much like Folkestone itself.

Dickens returned in 1855, this time renting 3 Albion Villas, high on the cliffs, for the whole summer. The house has now been renamed Copperfield House, and it was here that he worked on *Little Dorrit*. "a very pleasant little house with the sea below and the scent of thyme sweetening the breezes from the downs."

In October of that year he wrote to another friend: "I am going to read the "Carol" here to-morrow in a long carpenter's shop, which looks far more alarming as a place to hear in than the Town Hall at Birmingham." He was, of course, referring to his book *A Christmas Carol.*

Dickens' stays in Dover were longer than those in Folkestone, and he came on his own and with friends. He loved Paris, and no doubt found the easy crossing a great plus point, although he didn't seem to be very fond of the town itself.

In *The Uncommercial Traveller* he wrote: "I particularly detest Dover for the self-complacency with which it goes to bed. It always goes to bed (when I am going to Calais) with a more brilliant display of lamp and candle than any other town." "As I wait here on board the night packet, for the South-Eastern Train to come down with the Mail, Dover appears to me to be illuminated for some intensely aggravating festivity in my personal dishonour. All its noises smack of taunting praises of the land, and dispraises of the gloomy sea, and of me for going on it. The drums upon the heights have gone to bed, or I know they would rattle taunts against me for having my unsteady footing on this slippery deck. The many gas eyes of the Marine Parade twinkle in an offensive manner, as if with derision. "

Dover is described in *A Tale of Two Cities* as "A little mean crooked place which hid itself away from the beach and ran its head into the chalk cliffs like a marine ostrich."

Dickens used Dover as the backdrop to much of the action in David Copperfield. A plaque in Dickens Corner, 7 Market Square reads:"Here, while searching for his aunt Betsy Trotwood, David Copperfield rested on the doorstep and ate the loaf he had just bought." The shop was Igglesden's bakery and is now a café called The Market Square Kitchen. In the book, a fly driver directs Copperfield up to The Western Heights, where he finds his aunt's cottage in Pilot's Meadow. *'A very neat little cottage with cheerful bow windows: in front of it, a square gravelled court or garden full of flowers; carefully tended and smelling deliciously.'*

In 1852 Dickens stayed at 10 Camden Crescent, Dover, with his family, while continuing his manuscript for *Bleak House*. It was during this time that Wilkie Collins stayed with him. The place was destroyed in World War II, but a blue plaque marks the place, noting that the house where Dickens stayed was 'nearby'.

He wrote to Mrs Mary Boyle "It is not quite a place to my taste, being too bandy (I mean musical, no reference to its legs), and infinitely too genteel. But the sea is very fine, and the walks are quite remarkable. There are two ways of going to Folkestone, both lovely and striking in the highest degree; and there are heights, and downs, and country roads, and I don't know what, everywhere." Both routes would have been about seven or eight miles, one taking a route across the downs and one following the line of the coast.

In the May of 1856, Dickens spent three days in Dover, but found that the bustle of the dock area interfered with his writing. "I had scarcely fallen into my most promising attitude, and dipped my pen in the ink, when I found the clock upon the pier – a red-faced clock with a white rim – importuning me in a highly vexatious manner to consult my watch, and see how I was off for Greenwich time. Having no intention of making a voyage or taking an observation, I had not the least need of Greenwich time, and could have put up with watering-place time as a sufficiently accurate article. The pier-clock, however, persisting, I felt it necessary to lay down my pen, compare my watch with him, and fall into a grave solicitude about half-seconds. I had taken up my pen again, and was about to commence that valuable chapter, when a Custom-house cutter under the window requested that I would hold a naval review of her, immediately. It was impossible, under the circumstances, for any mental resolution, merely human, to dismiss the Custom-house cutter, because the shadow of her topmast fell upon my paper, and the vane played on the masterly blank chapter."

A Tale of Two Cities starts with a coach journey to Dover. Dickens wrote: "The beach was a desert of heaps of sea and stones tumbling wildly about, and the sea did what it liked, and what it liked was destruction. It thundered at the town and thundered at the cliffs, and brought the coast down madly."

Dickens gives us an indication that smuggling was still very much a continuing affair when he writes: "A little fishing was done in the port and a quantity of strolling about by night, and looking seaward, particularly at those times when the tide made and was near flood. Small tradesmen who did no business whatever, sometimes unaccountably realised large fortunes and it were remarkable that nobody in the neighbourhood could endure a lamplighter!"

In 1861 Dickens stayed in both Dover and Folkestone, and we are lucky he was such an enthusiastic letter-writer, as we have details of much of his time here.

> "Of course I am dull and penitent here, but it is very beautiful. I can work well, and I walked, by the cliffs, to Folkestone and back to-day, when it was so exquisitely beautiful that, though I was alone, I could not keep silence on the subject. In the fourteen miles I doubt if I met twelve people."

Maidstone was just over ten miles south of Gadd's Hill, and eight miles from Rochester. As the county town, it will have been very familiar to Dickens, and is immortalised as the town of Muggleton in *The Pickwick Papers*, appearing in 1836 when the members met at The Blue Lion Pub.

'There was an open square for the market-place; and in the centre of it, a large inn with a sign-post in front, displaying an object very common in art, but rarely met with in nature - to wit, a blue lion, with three bow legs in the air, balancing himself on the extreme point of the centre claw of his fourth foot.'

Followers of Dicken will be quick to recognise The White Lion in Maidstone town centre, but others have identified it as The Swan in West Malling with Cob Tree Hall representing Manor Farm, home of Mr. Wardle and family where the Pickwickians spend Christmas

Despite being the seat of the Anglican Church, Canterbury is often overlooked by those who travel to Kent, who often prefer the bustle of the larger towns or the picturesque nature of the coastal villages.

In *David Copperfield*, you can feel the weight of the history that pervades all aspects of the town. Dickens writes about "the shadows of the venerable gateways and churches". He reimagines The King's School as Dr Strong's School - "a grave building in a courtyard with a learned air about it", and The House of Agnes, in St Dunstans Street, near Canterbury West Station that is now a hotel – becomes the home of Agnes Wickfield.

Lastly, mentioning just one more of the many places Dickens visited and even stayed at in Canterbury, one cannot fail but mention the crooked Sir John Boyes House in Palace Street - "a very old house bulging out over the road...leaning forward, trying to see who was passing on the narrow pavement below."

Dickens was also a regular visitor to Deal, which was a much more important town than it is today. In 1850 he wrote:

> "Yesterday Charles Knight, White, Forster, Charley, and I walked to Richborough Castle and back. This is a distance of ten miles."

Dickens also passed through it on his long walks from Broadstairs to Dover and back to Fort House. He used the town in his novel *Bleak House*, for its proximity to The Downs offshore mooring spot and its use as a sea port.

"At last we came into the narrow streets of Deal, and very gloomy they were upon a raw misty morning. The long flat beach, with its little irregular houses, wooden and brick, and its litter of capstans, and great boats, and sheds, and bare upright poles with tackle and blocks, and loose gravelly waste places overgrown with grass and weeds, wore as dull an appearance as any place I ever saw."

Dickens used many other locations in his books, and surely travelled to many more than we will ever hear about. Dingly Dell, for example, which features in *The Pickwick Papers* is said to be based on Sandling. He particularly loved the northern-most reaches of the county, walking miles on the marshes across the Hoo peninsular.

He writes in *Great Expectations*: "The marshes were just a long black horizontal line ... the river was just another horizontal line, not nearly so broad nor yet so black, and the sky was just a row of long angry red lines and dense black lines intermingled"

He was also particularly fond of Cobham, four miles from his home at Gads Hill. It was in Cobham that went to The Leather Bottle Inn, and found it so much to his liking that it featured several times in *The Pickwick Papers.*

At Shorne, the graveyard of St Peter and St Paul church is mentioned in *The Pickwick Papers* and described by Dickens as a place where "...the soft landscape around forms the fairest spot in the garden of England."

Dickens was fond of the seclusion and peace offered by graveyards, and St James' churchyard in Cooling is one of those. The children's gravestones immortalised by Dickens in *Great Expectations* still bring an emotional response from visitors, who can imagine Magwitch hiding behind the gravestones while waiting for Pip

Graves at the Church of St James, Cooling

21

Arthur Conan Doyle

(1859-1930)

Sir Arthur Ignatius Conan Doyle is more often than not referred to as Arthur Conan Doyle or just Conan Doyle. In fact, Conan is one of his middle names, and the only surname which appears on his birth certificate is Doyle. His name is inseparable from that of his creation, the detective Sherlock Holmes.

Doyle moved to Crowborough, East Sussex in 1903, when he was 44 and became a regular visitor to various locations in Kent. It was in Crowborough that he suffered a heart attack and died. However, he is not buried there, but in Hampshire, according to the wishes of his wife.

Groombridge Place, near Tunbridge Wells, is just on the border of Kent and East Sussex, and has a strong connection to the writer. Doyle was a frequent guest at the house, and his Baker Street study has been re-created in the house. When in Kent, Doyle was particularly fond of the Groombridge garden, and he liked to sit in the so-called Drunken Garden, which was given its name from the haphazard topiary shapes created in the trees. The house was the setting for *The Valley of Fear* (1915), and Birlstone Manor is based on the house itself, described by Conan Doyle as a Jacobean brick house surrounded by a "beautiful broad moat, as still and luminous as quicksilver in the cold winter sunshine."

Dr Watson recalls:

> "I took a stroll in the curious old-world garden which flanked the house. Rows of very ancient yew trees cut into strange designs girded it round. Inside was a beautiful stretch of lawn with an old sundial in the middle, the whole effect so soothing and restful that it was welcome to my somewhat jangled nerves.
>
> ...
>
> I have said that a decoration of yew trees circled the garden. At the end, farthest from the house they thickened into a continuous hedge. On the other side of this hedge, concealed from the eyes of anyone approaching from the direction of the house, there was a stone seat..."

Doyle used his knowledge of Kentish places to create scenes such as The Cedars in Lee, home of Neville Saint-Clair, in *The Man with the Twisted Lip*, and Yoxley Old Place, Chatham, (seven miles from Chatham and three from the railway line). He was fond of large houses, and also created Abbey Grange, in the fictional village of Marsham, for *The Greek Interpreter* and Popham House, again near Lee, as the home of John Scott Eccles.

In all, Doyle set eight of his stories in Kent towns and villages. It was the coming of the railway which allowed him to travel freely, and he was much taken with the beauty of the countryside through which he travelled and which features in the stories. In *The Return of Sherlock Holmes,* the story *The Adventure of the Golden Pince-Nez*is set in Chatham.

The Adventure of the Final Problem briefly features Canterbury, when Sherlock Holmes and Dr Watson make a quick stop in the city, merely getting off one train and onto another.

The Crooked House, Canterbury

22

Michael Drayton

(1563-1631)

Poet Michael Drayton was born in Warwickshire, but deserves to be included in a book about Kentish writers because of his wonderful descriptions of the county in his poem *Poly-Olbion*, which he wrote towards the end of his career in 1612. Having written in many different genres throughout his life, this epic poem was a culmination of all that he had learnt, presenting a vivid picture of the landscape and legends of England at the time.

We know that Drayton had been working on the 15,000 line poem for at least fifteen years, and that it was his masterpiece.

Presented in two volumes, the work is divided into songs instead of verses, and describes the various counties of England in turn. The volumes included thirty maps by William Hole and illustrations by John Seddon.

Song 18 is devoted to Kent, and like the other songs, views the county from the perspective of the rivers. The affections of the Rother River are vied for by the Isle of Oxney and Romney Marsh, and The Medway and The Thames join together to sing the praises of Norman warriors. Also described in detail are The Isle of Sheppey, The Isle of Grain and The Isle of Thanet. The other main Kentish River, the River Stour also features as a strong voice in the poem.

> ......, " O famous Kent !
> What county hath this isle that can compare with thee?
> That hath within thyself as much as thou can'st wish:
> Thy rabbits, venison, fruits, thy sorts of fowl and fish:
> As what with strength comports, thy hay, thy corn, thy wood, -
> Nor anything doth want that anywhere is good."

23

George Eliot

(1819-1880)

Mary Ann Evans is a novelist perhaps best-known for *The Mill on the Floss, Silas Marner* and *Middlemarch,* but she also worked as a journalist and translator and wrote poetry. Her pen name was George Eliot, chosen to avoid any discrimination against women writers.

While staying in Broadstairs in the summer of 1852, she wrote to a friend saying, “I warn you against Ramsgate which is a strip of London come out for an airing,” but described Broadstairs as “perfect”.

As the Broadstairs railway had not yet been built, Eliot would have travelled either by train as far as Whitstable, and by horse-drawn coach from there to her lodgings, or by steam packet, alighting at Steamer Point, at the end of the Broadstairs pier.

She rented Chandos Cottage consisting of one small sitting room and a bedroom, on the corner of Oscar Road and Chandos Road, paying a guinea a week. She liked it so much that she wrote "I am thinking whether it would not be wise to retire from the world and live here for the rest of my days." Sadly for us, she never did.

Later that same month, she wrote to another friend "I thought of you last night when I was in a state of mingled rapture and torture – rapture at the sight of a glorious evening sky, torture at the sight and hearing of the belabouring given to the poor donkey which was drawing me from Ramsgate home." The donkey cart would have held a maximum of two people and travelled the two miles between Ramsgate and Broadstairs on a regular basis.

In the end, she stayed for two months, enjoying everything the little town had to offer. It was unusual for a single woman to holiday on her own, so she was accompanied to the lodgings by some married friends. As it happened, there was still a scandal, as she wrote to Herbert Spencer to ask him to meet her in the town. He came a few weeks later and booked himself into a nearby hotel. The romance was doomed, however, and Spencer finally told her that he was not in love with her as she was with him.

The story ended happily, however, as she continued the holiday alone picking up shells, visiting and reading Henry Lewes's new novel *Rose, Blanche and Violet*. She was dismissive of the work, but their friendship deepened, and it was Henry who turned out to be the love of her life, not Herbert Spencer.

Eliot also stayed in Dover, as many travellers to and from the continent did, while waiting for a ship or just to break their journey and recover from the sea voyage. In 1855, on her way back from Germany, Eliot stayed in Athol Terrace. The buildings, pressed up against the white cliffs, had been specifically designed for travellers and overlook the harbour. She was not idle during her stay, and writes in her journal:

> "As I walked up the Castle hill this afternoon, the town, with its background of softly rounded hills shrouded in sleepy haze, its little lines of water looking golden in the sun, made a charming picture."

Botany Bay, Thanet

24

TS Eliot

(1888-1965)

One of the least picturesque parts of the Margate seafront is the shelter which looks out over the sea. Surprisingly, this unprepossessing, utilitarian block of glass and iron is a Grade II listed building, known as being the place where poet Thomas Stearns Eliot chose to relax while he penned a few verses of his poem *The Wasteland*.

In 1921 Eliot came to stay at The Albermarle Hotel in Cliftonville while he recovered from a nervous breakdown, and he liked to sit in solitude watching the sea. The Albermarle, now long gone was on The Eastern Esplanade, between Harold Road and

Norfolk Road, with views over The Oval Gardens to the sea. An advertisement of the time boasts that it is 'replete with every comfort' while at the same time having a 'modest tariff'. During his stay, Eliot would take the tram to the far end of Margate Sands, a mile and a half a way and use the Nayland Rock shelter to protect himself from the winds.

The poem he struggled with, published a year later, was 'The Wasteland'. The work is generally regarded as one of the finest of the twentieth century, reflecting on the state of society after The First World War.

Having been granted three months' sick leave, he wrote to a friend that he was out all day apart from when he was resting, and mentioned sitting in the shelter. He also spent time sketching and playing the mandolin, a popular instrument at the time.

A decade later, Eliot's connection with the county renewed. He was asked to write a play for The Canterbury Festival, and chose the story of Thomas Becket. The play was, of course, *Murder in the Cathedral* and was first performed in the Chapter House of Canterbury Cathedral in 1935 before moving to London.

25

Ian Fleming

(1908-1964)

Ian Lancaster Fleming was an author and journalist who will be forever linked with his most famous character, James Bond. He worked for the Naval Intelligence Division during the Second World War, and drew on these experiences for his novels.

After the war, Fleming secured a job as a journalist, but was able to take three months off each winter, which he chose to spend in Jamaica, where he became friendly with Noel Coward. He stepped down from full-time work in 1959.

Fleming visited Coward in Kent, staying at a now-demolished hotel in Sandwich. He eventually bought a house near Coward, and in 1952 purchased Coward's own house White Cliffs in St Margaret's Bay. Coincidentally, Fleming's character James Bond was gifted a holiday home in St Margaret's Bay by his creator.

The two friends often went to The Granville pub in St Margarets, now demolished, but immortalised in *Moonraker* as The Granville Hotel.

He moved from there to The Old Palace in Bekesbourne, which is near to Higham, home of Count Louis Zborowski. The count was a keen creator and racer of fast cars, and it was his car nicknamed Chitty Bang Bang that inspired Fleming's children's story *Chitty Chitty Bang Bang*. Fleming knew the east of Kent well, and The Goodwin Sands appear in the story as the setting for the picnic on the sand. The book was not published in Fleming's lifetime, but came to the market two months after his death.

The character James Bond had his childhood home in Pett Bottom, in a cottage next door to The Duck pub owned by his Aunt Charmian, who brought him up after his parents died in a climbing accident. The cottage is real, and has now become part of the pub. Fleming was fond of The Duck, and it was there that he wrote much of *You Only Live Twice* (1964), including references to the pub in which he sat.

The novel *Moonraker*, published in 1955, is set wholly in the UK, and Kent, of course, appears in many scenes, including the location of Moonraker's research lab 'on the edge of the cliffs between Dover and Deal'. After the landslide, Bond and Brand swim beneath the White Cliffs of Dover. Later, Bond drives north out of Dover, past ‘the wonderful cardboard castle’. Bond also passed through Aldington and travelled through Romney Marsh.

Pegwell Bay and Kingsdown are both mentioned in the book. *Goldfinger* had a mansion near Reculver, to which he invited James Bond, and even Goldfinger’s company, based in Ramsgate, gives a nod to the area, being called Thanet Alloys.

From 1957-1959, Fleming lived at The Old Palace in Bekesbourne and between 1961 and 1964 rented apartments in Pegwell Bay, Manston Airport, Folkestone, Leeds Castle and Sandwich. Fleming’s character Hugo Drax drives through Maidstone, passing King Street and Gabriel’s Hill, stopping later at The Thomas Wyatt Hotel. Maidstone also features in *The Man with the Golden Gun*, when Bond goes to a firing range there.

Fleming was very fond of golf, and one of the main attractions of East Kent was the Royal St George’s Golf Club at Sandwich and he was elected Captain for the 1964/5 season. The club becomes Royal St Marks in the novel *Goldfinger*, where Bond and Auric Goldfinger play a round. Each hole played is recognisable as a hole at St George’s.

Fleming suffered a fatal heart attack while in Kent and died in the county he loved. He was staying in Canterbury, in the summer of 1964, and had been to The Royal St George’s Golf club. He collapsed one evening and he died the next morning at The Kent and Canterbury Hospital, aged just 56. Although he died in Kent, an area which he loved, he is buried in Wiltshire near his family home of Sevenhampton.

26

Ford Madox Ford

(1873-1939)

Ford Hermann Hueffer was the grandson of the painter Ford Madox Brown, after whom he was named. He used the name Ford Hueffer until after The First World War, when, like many other British families with German heritage, he decided to anglicise his name.

He was born and brought up in Surrey, and was sent to The Praetorius School in Folkestone until 1889 when his father died and he was moved to London.

At the age of 20 he eloped with Elsie Martindale and started family life in Kent, where he formed a close friendship with Joseph Conrad and also became acquainted with Henry James, Stephen Crane, and H. G. Wells. The couple rented a farmhouse in Bonnington, in a remote house called Bloomfield Villa which has now been renamed Fir Trees Villa, where Elsie gave birth to their two daughters. Ford described the village in *Return to Yesterday*, published in 1931 as a remote place developed from common land to be tiny independent plots surrounded by hawthorn hedges.

By the time the author was 24, he had published a novel, a biography, several poems and three collections of fairy tales.

His connections with other writers and the friendship with Conrad especially, grew and the friends collaborated on several writing projects. In 1898, Conrad and his family moved into Pent Farmhouse, rented by Ford, and the Ford family moved to a property nearby.

The Fords only stayed there for three years and in 1901 they moved to Winchelsea in East Sussex.

Ford's most recognisably Kentish poem is Aldington Knoll, based on the legend of a giant who is buried near the village.

27

Caroline Fry

(1787-1846)

Theologian and writer Caroline Wilson, as she was known after her marriage, was a true Kentish Maid, being born in Tunbridge Wells and living in the county all her life. John Fry, Caroline's farmer father, died when she was 14, but had printed at his own cost some copies of her verses The History of England, which his daughter had written in the schoolroom and he had admired.

Fry attended school in London from the age of 17, for just over a year and then took up residence with a respectable family in Bloomsbury, where she could be introduced into society. She stayed with the family for three years, but may not have found the frivolities of high society to her taste, having been brought up in a restricted high church home.

Fry had first been published professionally the year before her marriage in 1824, when she started to write for *The Assistant of Education, Religious and Literary.* This was a periodical magazine designed to educate children on religious matters, which she wrote and edited herself.

In addition to writing the magazine, Fry wrote prayers, poetry and what might be termed 'uplifting moral tales', which recounted the lives of people she had met and found influential. These were published in two volumes entitled *The Listener.* After its first appearance in 1830, the work continued in publication through several editions and was published in America in 1863, and France in 1844.

She also wrote her own autobiography, describing her conversion experience in 1822.

After her marriage, Fry continued to write on religious themes, including hymns and prayers. Of her hymns the best known are 'For what shall I praise Thee, my God and my King,' and 'Often the clouds of deepest woe.'

28

Charles Hamilton

(1876-1961)

London-born Charles Harold St John Hamilton used the pen name Frank Richards for his stories about Greyfriars School, and is best known for the character Billy Bunter.

After leaving full-time education aged 17, Charles embarked upon a career as a novelist, and had his first story published in 1895.

The stories of Billy Bunter and his adventures at Greyfriars School were published in 'The Magnet' from 1908 until 1940. From 1947, fans were able to buy the stories in hardback book form. The stories were later enjoyed by generations of children as radio, television and stage productions.

The fictional Greyfriars School “pleasantly situated near the south coast of Kent”, was perched on the banks of the River Sark near the villages of Friardale and Courtfield, which are also fictional.

Many of the towns mentioned in Hamilton’s stories are, of course, real places. He includes ‘merry Margate’ which he describes as the ‘brightest and jolliest place on the East Coast’, home of the Dreamland Entertainment Park, North Foreland Lighthouse and many more.

Billy Bunter also visits Dover and amusingly, refers to the Cinque Ports as the Sunk Ports.

The way of life at the schools and the characters portrayed have come under recent criticism for their elitism and right-wing ethics, but are now generally regarded as a historically accurate representation of the world at the time they were written and can be regarded as a ‘period piece’.

Hamilton’s first stay in Kent was in 1914. He was working as a war correspondent and rented rooms above the Post Office in the village of Hawkinge, now home to the Kent Battle of Britain Museum, the largest of its kind in the world.

The writer moved permanently to Kent in 1926, aged 50. He lived in the same house, Rose Lawn at 131 Percy Avenue, Kingsgate, near Broadstairs for over 30 years until his death in 1961. He never married, but was looked after by his loyal housekeeper Edith Hood. The house is still standing, and has a blue plaque showing the name Frank Richards. It no longer backs onto cornfields as it did when he lived there, but it does run down to the sea, where Hamilton would sit and ponder the details of his next story.

Despite the popularity of Billy Bunter, he was not Hamilton's only creation. He used 25 other pen names, including Owen Conquest and Martin Clifford, and wrote about two other boys schools, Rookwood and St Jims, as well as publishing under his own name. He also tried other genres, notably romance, which were published under the pen name Winston Cardew, and he wrote detective stories, westerns and adventures in a range of other settings.

Hamilton wrote continuously throughout his life, producing an over 70,000 words a week, and it is estimated that his output equalled over 1,000 full-length novels. He is listed in The Guinness Book of World Records as the world's most prolific writer.

29

F Hodgson Burnett

(1849-1924)

Children's author Frances Eliza Hodgson was born in Manchester, but moved to America with her parents when she was 16. She started her literary career by submitting short stories to magazines and periodicals.

After her divorce in 1898 she moved back to England, and rented Great Maytham Hall, half a mile outside the tiny village of Rolvenden, about three miles south-west of Tenterden. The hall was a large house with a magnificent walled garden and a tower from which she could see The English Channel. It had recently suffered from a fire, and been repaired just enough to be rented out. She loved the house, which, to her, represented the true spirit of England and wrote that “it is the only place I ever felt was home”.

The Little Princess was published in 1904, but Burnett returned to America in 1907 before writing *The Secret Garden*. However, there is no doubt that Maytham Hall was the inspiration for the book which has so delighted generations of children. The book was initially serialised in a magazine, and received mixed reviews, but its popularity has endured whereas the appeal of more immediately popular works has faded.

The garden had been neglected for years when she arrived, and she threw herself enthusiastically into its restoration, clearing weeds and planting roses. Once restored, she described it as "a lovesome, mystic place, shut in partly by old red brick walls… it was my habit to sit and write there under an aged writhen tree, grey with lichen and festooned with roses."

In her book, *In the Garden*, she wrote, “I love it all. I love to dig. I love to kneel down in the grass at the edge of a flower bed and pull out the weeds fiercely and throw them into a heap by my side. I love to fight with those who can spring up again almost in a night and taunt me.”

The gazebo-covered seating area which she created became an outdoor sanctuary where she could plan and write some of her many books. She was by no means a recluse, however, joining in with local events and hosting visitors at the hall as well as taking regular trips both within the UK and abroad. Her guests included Ellen Terry, Henry James and Rudyard Kipling, who all lived nearby. Rolvenden railway station was opened in

1900, about two miles from Maytham Hall, and offered travel to Robertsbridge in East Sussex, Headcorn to the north, and all stations in between.

Burnett was a prolific author, and produced fifty-two novels and thirteen plays as well as her popular children's literature. When she moved to Rolvenden, she was already a celebrity, as popular in her day as any contemporary children's author.

Great Maytham Hall has since been divided into apartments, but reception rooms are available as a wedding venue and the walled garden has been preserved. The garden can be seen by appointment or during the National Garden Scheme's Open Gardens Week.

30

Charles Igglesden

(1861-1949)

Kentish man Charles Igglesden was born into a family of entrepreneurs. His grandfather, William Igglesden, had businesses as estate agents, furniture removers, and funeral directors, amongst others. The family is best known locally as the architects of The Kentish Express newspaper, which Charles' father Henry started in 1855.

Igglesden took over as editor of The Kentish Express in his turn, but was also a keen writer and amateur artist. He loved to walk, and created a series of articles under the title *A Saunter Through Kent with Pen and Pencil*, in which he visited hundreds of Kentish villages. The articles were later collated into over 30 hardback books which were available from 1899 until 1944. The series was recently updated with a posthumous 35th volume in 2018

It is interesting to follow the Igglesden family through the data from the National Census.

Igglesden is shown on the 1861 census at 2 months old living with his parents and two siblings in the shop on Ashford High Street. His father is a Newspaper Proprietor and Bookseller, and they live with two house servants and two assistant booksellers.

By 1871 the family live at 24 East Hill, now Northbrook House, on the Canterbury to Ashford road. The business has gone well, and Igglesden's father employs an further four men and an additional nine boys. Igglesden has a little sister, and his grandmother and aunt have moved in with them. They employ two house servants.

By 1891 Igglesden has married and is head of his own household, and is listed on the census as a Newspaper Proprietor in his own right. The family continue to move, first to Oakwood House and then to Heathfield, on the Canterbury Road. On the 1901 census, we see the word 'author' inserted beside Igglesden's occupation as newspaper proprietor.

Although best known for his saunters books, Igglesden also wrote 13 novels and several books on cricket. Xavier Willis, who illustrated the books, shared his enthusiasm for cricket. Some of Igglesdsen's best-known works are *A History of the East Kent Rifle Volunteers*, and his cricketing stories.

The Hubert Fountain, Victoria Park, Ashford

31

Ben Jonson

(1572-1637)

Benjamin Jonson was born in 1572 and was one of the foremost poets of the Elizabethan period.

He was a regular visitor to Penshurst Place, five miles west of Tonbridge, where he stayed with Robert Sydney, Sir Philip Sydney and met the diarist John Evelyn.

Johnson's poem 'To Penshurst', which was written in the first decade of the eighteenth century, and 'The Forest' are testament to how familiar he was with the area.

Now, Penshurst, they that will proportion thee
With other edifices, when they see
Those proud, ambitious heaps, and nothing else,
May say their lords have built, but thy lord dwells.

The detailed description gives an impression of a place of dreamy, sylvan perfection, apart from normal life, a paradise of plenty and hospitality for owners, servants and visitors alike.

Then hath thy orchard fruit, thy garden flowers,
Fresh as the air, and new as are the hours.
The early cherry, with the later plum,
Fig, grape, and quince, each in his time doth come;
The blushing apricot and woolly peach
Hang on thy walls, that every child may reach.
And though thy walls be of the country stone,
They're reared with no man's ruin, no man's groan;
There's none that dwell about them wish them down;
But all come in, the farmer and the clown,
And no one empty-handed, to salute
Thy lord and lady, though they have no suit.

Jonson references Kent in 'The Progresses, Progressions and Magnificent Festivities of King James'… in which he describes preposterous things:

As for example, a belly and no face,
With the bill of a shoveller may here come in place
The haunches of a drum with the feet of a pot
And the tail of a Kentishman to it; why not?

The suggestion that Kentishmen have tails is a reference to the legend that while travelling through Strood, Robert de Broc cut off the tail of Thomas Becket's horse, and that Becket then cursed the people of Strood with the prediction that their children would all be born with tails.

32

John Keats

(1795-1821)

The poet John Keats was born in London, and in his short twenty-five-year life, wrote poetry that has had a lasting effect on the literary world. His poems *Ode to Autumn* and *Ode to a Nightingale* are staples on the school curriculum.

In 1816, aged 21 and still coming to terms with his artistic abilities, Keats had recently qualified to practise as an apothecary, and had enrolled as a student at Guy's Hospital in London, studying on the job to become a surgeon.

He was at a junction in his life, vacillating between the desire to practise medicine and the feeling that he should become a full-time poet. He took the opportunity to assess his direction by travelling with his brother Thomas to Margate.

It was here that he wrote 'To Charles Cowden Clarke' and 'Epistle to My Brother George', which includes these lines about the ocean, encapsulating the feelings of many of us who look upon the vastness of the sea:

"The ocean with its vastness, its blue green,
Its ships, its rocks, its caves, its hopes, its fears,—
Its voice mysterious, which whoso hears
Must think on what will be, and what has been."

Keats stayed for two months, enjoying the summer sun in what was then a very fashionable place to be.

The next year, he returned to Kent, staying once more in the town of Margate, having written the first lines of 'Endymion' on The Isle of Wight and become stagnated. He lived in Margate from April to May of 1817, hoping that a stay in his previous lodgings would help, explaining in a letter to Leigh Hunt that he "*... set off pell-mell for Margate, at least 150 Miles, because, forsooth, I fancied that I should like my old Lodging here, and could contrive to do without Trees."* The fact that Thanet has very few trees is well-known, and was obviously observed first-hand by Keats.

He was joined by his brother again, and the pair soon left for Canterbury, although there is no evidence of where or how long his visit lasted. We do know that he was hoping the spirit of Chaucer would help him to write and that he was back in London by June, before leaving the country in 1820 on what would be his last journey, to Italy. Interestingly, his journey to Italy was taken by sea, and Keats stopped once more in Kent, if only briefly, on his journey.

It was September 1820 when the Keats left London with his friend Joseph Severn. Their ship, *Maria Crowther*, travelled down The Thames and round the whole coast of Kent before stopping at Portsmouth. She then sailed south towards The Mediterranean Sea, after a journey of six weeks, docking at Naples.

The first night on board was spent moored offshore at Gravesend. Keats took the opportunity to go ashore and buy some things from a chemist, as well as '1/2 hundred apples and 2 Dozen Biscuits' – a fitting remembrance of the county of Kent.

33

Rudyard Kipling

(1865-1936)

Joseph Rudyard Kipling was born in India wrote for both adults and children, with is book *Just So Stories* influencing many writers to this day. He travelled widely before settling in East Sussex in 1902. His house, Batemans, is less than ten miles from the border with Kent, and he had many friends in Kent with whom he stayed with on a regular basis, such as Frances Hodgson Burnett, who lived just 15 miles away at Maytham Hall.

He loved to walk in the woods and open countryside, and this is evident in his poem 'Brookland Road'; Brookland is a Kentish village about 15 miles from Batemans. It has been suggested that his poem 'The Way Through the Woods' was based on the Canterbury area, in particular the old road north towards Herne.

Kipling had certainly visited the area, as he opened a new building for Canterbury's Junior King's School at Milner Court, Sturry, in October 1929. The house had been bequeathed to the school by Lady Milner on the death of her husband, who was a close friend of Kipling. In 1925 she granted the 80-acre grounds, Tudor house and associated buildings to the school and the aptly named Sturry Court was renamed Milner Court. Included on the estate was a wooded island, reached by a distinctive bridge, which has recently been refurbished and opened up for use by the pupils.

Another Kentish link is found in Kipling's short story *The Dog Hervey*, included in the book *A Diversity of Creatures* (1917). He mentions the children's rhyme Little Bingo. Bingo appears in *The Lay of St Gengulphus*, one of *The Ingoldsby Legends*, written by Kentish author Richard Barham. The rhyme was not written by Barham, but he gives us the earliest written record of it. The reference in Kipling's story shows that he was familiar with the work as a whole.

> 'A franklyn's dogge leped over a style,
> And his name was littel Byngo!
> B wyth a Y -- Y wyth an N,
> N wyth a G -- G wyth an O --
> They call'd him little Byngo!

34

Jack London

(1876-1915)

John Griffith London, known as Jack, was an American writer , author of *White Fang* and *The Call of the Wild,* but also made a significant contribution to our understanding of the life of a hop picker when he visited Kent in 1903.

London had been staying in the capital, studying life in the slums, when he headed down The London Road towards Maidstone in search of work. On reaching the town, he took lodgings in the poorer quarter of the town.

His book *The People of the Abyss* was influenced predominantly by his stay in London, but also includes a chapter on the life of hop pickers in Kent. The book was read widely, and inspired, among others, George Orwell, who followed London's example and went into the poorest parts of London and the surrounding areas himself.

London makes some insightful comments about the hoppers who came to work in the fields. Particularly astute is his comment on the fact that they had been driven away from the land to find work in the cities, but when they returned to boost a shortage of local workers they 'return not as prodigals, but as outcast still, as vagrants and pariahs, to be doubted and flouted by their country brethren, to sleep in jails and casual wards, or under the hedges, and to live the Lord knows how.' This is especially true when the workers arrived before the hops were ready to be picked, and they had no means of making a living.

Later, London describes a storm which battered the unpicked hops, damaging them beyond redemption.

> "I passed through Teston and East and West Farleigh shortly after the storm, and listened to the grumbling of the hoppers and saw the hops rotting on the ground. At the hothouses of Barham Court, thirty thousand panes of glass had been broken by the hail, while peaches, plums, pears, apples, rhubarb, cabbages, mangolds, everything, had been pounded to pieces and torn to shreds."

He travelled with an East End cobbler, Bert, who, like London, dressed in his worst clothes for the occasion, to better assess the reception he would receive. They were shunned by the great and the good, but found that even their worst clothing was better than that of the hoppers.

The pair eventually found work, and set to it.

> We sat on the edge of the bin, between the standing hops, while a pole-puller supplied us with great fragrant branches. In an hour's time we became as expert as it is possible to become. As soon as the fingers became accustomed automatically to differentiate between hops and leaves and to strip half-a-dozen blossoms at a time there was no more to learn.
>
> As the afternoon wore along, we realised that living wages could not be made—by men. Women could pick as much as men, and children could do almost as well as women; so it was impossible for a man to compete with a woman and half-a-dozen children. For it is the woman and the half-dozen children who count as a unit, and by their combined capacity determine the unit's pay.

The two men found that they had not earnt enough to reach the minimum pay bracket, and left the field empty-handed. Luckily, they had brought money with them and walked into Maidstone for their dinner.

This one small addition to our knowledge of the hop-pickers' lives shows that sometimes an outside eye is needed to cast light on our own shortcomings.

35

Christopher Marlowe

(1564-1593)

Playwright Christopher Marlowe was born in the city of Canterbury and baptised at the church of St George the Martyr, near the modern Whitefriars Shopping Centre. Only the tower of the church now remains, bearing a memorial plaque to one of the most famous sons of the city.

He benefitted from an education at The King's School in Canterbury and then attended Cambridge University. Marlowe produced an extraordinary series of plays including *Tamburlaine, The Jew of Malta* and *Doctor Faustus*. His first play was published when he was just 22 years old.

Marlowe's poems include his retelling of the Greek myth of Hero and Leander. Several of his poems have sexual themes, and many have been identified as homo-erotic. His poem 'On the Death of Sir Roger Manwood' is an address to the judge who gives his name to a private school in Sandwich.

He wrote prolifically, and one of the most famous lines in English poetry is one attributed to Marlow: "Come live with me and be my love" is from 'The Passionate Shepherd to His Love', published posthumously in 1599.

It is assumed that he also led a double life as a spy for Elizabeth I, although there is tantalizingly little evidence for this. His religious views would have been cause for concern, as he read widely about both Roman Catholicism and atheism. If Marlowe had worked as a spy, he must have travelled repeatedly through Kent going to and from the continent.

At the age of 29 Marlowe was stabbed to death in Deptford, leaving a bewildered public to guess at the motive of the attack and decide whether it was an assassination or aggravated manslaughter. The court rolls show the skill of the lawyers, and Ingram Frizer who stabbed Kit, pleaded self-defence and was pardoned by the queen just two weeks later. It has been suggested that Frizer was also a spy and had either been engaged to kill Marlowe or to gather information from him.

Whatever the reason for his early death, there is little doubt that Kit Marlowe was one of the greatest playwrights of the era; Anthony Burgess' novel *A Dead Man in Deptford* reflects upon this incident.

He was buried in Deptford in St Nicholas Church, in an unmarked grave but a memorial stone has now been erected in the churchyard.

The Marlowe Theatre in central Canterbury is dedicated to the writer. Outside is The Marlowe Memorial installed in 1891 in The Buttermarket, near Canterbury Cathedral, but moved several times before finding its current home.

The bell tower of the church of St George the Martyr, Canterbury

36

Edith Nesbit

(1858-1924)

Edith Nesbit was born in Surrey, but her family lived in several English counties while she was a child, as well as spending time in France, Spain and Germany. She was known affectionately as Daisy to her family, and her children's books are known world-wide.

When they settled in England, the family chose Halstead, six miles north of Sevenoaks, and Edith spent three very happy years here, playing with her siblings in Halstead Hall, a red-brick house "that might have been commonplace but for the roses and the ivy that clung to the front of it and the rich heavy jasmine that covered the side" and watching the construction of the Chelsfield-Knockholt railway line. The station at Halstead-for-Knockholt, was later renamed Knockholt. The children must have been particularly interested in the construction of the cutting, which was to feature in her later novel, The Railway Children.

Edith's first works were for adults, but she is now best-known as a children's author. She began as a poet, writing for magazines and greetings cards, and after the success of some poems for children, was inspired to write twelve short stories. These later became the basis for *The Story of The Treasure Seekers*, (1898).

Once she found her love of writing for children, in her 40s, she completed upwards of 40 books, and her books *The Story of the Treasure Seekers* (1898) and *The Wouldbegoods* (1899), *Five Children and It* (1902), *The Phoenix and the Carpet* (1904), The Railway Children (1906), and *The Enchanted Castle* (1907*)*, are still favourites. Their popularity endures, and they have all been made into both films and TV series. She created idealized worlds for happy children, blotting out her own unhappy memories of constant moving and bullying at school, and the experiences of the families in her books did not reflect her own bohemian lifestyle.

The stories are rooted in the Kentish countryside, and the local influence can clearly be seen in *The Railway Children* where the story is set around Knockholt Station. In *The Phoenix and the Carpet*, too, Kentish folklore prevails, when the children delve into Richard Barham's Ingoldsby Legends for inspiration, and in *The Incredible Honeymoon* she says: If you go to Yalding you may stay at the George and be comfortable in a little village that owns a haunted churchyard, a fine church, and one of the most beautiful bridges in Europe.

The children's adventure books have been cited as the first of the genre, but she was also known for her supernatural stories. Her story *Man-size in Marble* is set in the church of St Eanswith in Brenzett, taking inspiration from the tomb of John Fagge and his son, which stands in The Lady Chapel.

In 1893, Edith and her first husband Hubert Bland moved to Dymchurch, and lived in several houses in the area. The place was a quiet fishing village at the time, although it is now a draw for tourists and has lost some of its charm. It was while they were living here that the couple became founding members of The Fabian Society and it was during this time that she claimed to have discovered a secret code proving that Francis Bacon wrote some of the plays attributed to William Shakespeare.

In 1917 she married for a second time and bought a house of two amalgamated cottages called The Long Boat and The Jolly Boat in Jesson, now known as St Mary's Bay, near New Romney. Nearby Nesbit Road is named for her. The house had started life as RAF Nissan huts, and now overlooks the Romney Hythe and Dymchurch Railway, the miniature railway which was the brain-child of Count Zbrowski, owner of Chitty Bang Bang (see Ian Fleming). The house was ideally suited for long walks or cycle rides under the open skies of the Romney Marsh, and for visits to her friend Noel Coward, who lived just two miles away.

Edith died in 1924 and is buried in the local church of St Mary in the Marsh. Her gravestone gives both her married name, Edith Bland, and the name by which she is most usually known, Edith Nesbit. It was carved from wood by her husband Thomas

'Skipper' Tucker. She particularly wanted to be buried under the spreading canopy of a large elm tree. Her wishes were carried out, but sadly the tree fell prey to Dutch Elm Disease in the 1970s. There is also a memorial to her inside the church.

As a postscript to her life, the 2009 novel *The Children's Book* by A.S.Byatt is loosely based on Nesbit's life, and as such is set in Dungeness and other parts of Kent.

Yalding Bridge

37

Emmuska Orczy

(1865-1947)

Baroness Emma Magdolna Rozália Mária Jozefa Borbála Orczy de Orci was born in Hungary and moved to the UK as a 14-year-old in 1880. She married Henry Barstow in 1894 and worked as a translator and illustrator to supplement the couple's income. Shortly after the birth of her son in 1899, she started to write fiction.

Orczy created one of the most well-known characters in British literature, *The Scarlet Pimpernel*. This was the alter-ego of Sir Peter Blakeney, who lived the life of a wealthy playboy by day but by night became the dashing hero helping members of the

French aristocracy to cross The English Channel and escape The French Revolution. The character was one of the first instances of a hero with a secret identity, which has now become such a staple of popular culture.

Oczy herself writes:

> "They seek him here, they seek him there,
> Those Frenchies seek him everywhere.
> Is he in heaven? Or is he in hell?
> That damned elusive Pimpernel!"

The Scarlet Pimpernel features in over a dozen books, working at night in the Romney Marsh area and eventually drawing around him The League of the Scarlet Pimpernel. Taking on a disguise, he outwits those who hope to thwart him, and leaves a scarlet pimpernel flower at the scene of his triumphs as a calling card. The scarlet pimpernel is a flower which is found on Romney Marsh, an area famed for its smuggling connections with the continent, so it is assumed that this is the base of Blakeney's operations. He also makes several trips from Dover, a port that the Baroness would have known well from her trips to mainland Europe.

A prolific writer, she also produced several romance novels and some mystery thrillers.

In 1908 the Baroness rented Cleve Court near Acol, just south of Birchington-on-Sea where she completed *Beau Brocade* and wrote *The Nest of the Sparrowhawk*, which is set in Acol during the 17th century.

She only stayed in the house for two years, after which she moved to Snowfield, Yeoman's Green, and Bearsted, which she remodelled extensively, adding a garden house in matching style. In 1912 she also added a house called Little Snowfield to the estate, for her mother. When her mother returned to Hungary, The Baroness moved to the smaller house herself and stayed for several years before moving to Monte Carlo, Monaco.

In recognition of her importance to British literature, the new Snowfield Estate includes a Pimpernel Close and a Blakeney Close.

Orczy later returned to England, ending her days in London.

38

George Orwell

(1903-1950)

Author of *1984* and *Animal Farm,* Eric Arthur Blair was born in India, and wrote under the pen name George Orwell. He travelled widely, living in different parts of India, France and the UK. He also spent two separate periods in Kent, for very different reasons.

In 1931, during the depression years between the two World Wars, Orwell kept a diary while going 'on the tramp' in London and Kent, earning a living by picking crops, most notably harvesting hops at Home Farm in Wateringbury and/or Blest's farm in West Malling – the details for each farm are very similar.

He lived in a traditional hoppers hut (which Orwell describes as 'worse than a stable' and worked alongside the families of the East End of London who had come to the county for a 'working holiday'. The text of these diaries can be found online on the site of The Orwell Foundation.

He used his knowledge to produce an essay called, unsurprisingly, 'Hop-picking' which was printed in 'The New Statesman' in 1931, and one of his novels which drew heavily on these experiences is *A Clergyman's Daughter* (1935). He describes hop-pickings as:

> " ... a life that wore you out, used up every ounce of your energy, and kept you profoundly, unquestionably happy. In the literal sense of the word, it stupefied you ... Your wits seemed to thicken, just as your skin did, in the rain and sunshine and perpetual fresh air."

The novel tells the story of Dorothy Hare, who after suffering a bout of amnesia, joins a group of friends in a journey to Kent for the hop-picking season. Orwell was never satisfied with it, and was reluctant for it to be published.

Orwell's second major excursion to Kent was in 1938, when he was admitted to Preston Hall Sanatorium, Aylesford suffering from tuberculosis. The hospital had been set up in 1925 by The British Legion for the treatment of ex-servicemen, and went on to become the corner-stone of the British Legion Village. Although Orwell himself had not been in the army, the hospital did take a few civilian patients, and as Orwell's brother-in-law was a surgeon at the hospital, this may have paved his way.

Orwell stayed in Aylesford for six months, recuperating at the hospital, benefitting from a private room and access to the large, well-maintained gardens. There was a Home Farm attached to the hospital where Orwell is known to have worked.

39

William Pett Ridge

(1859-1930)

William Pett Ridge's parents James and Elizabeth Ridge were both born in Devon, but James' job as a station master soon meant a move out of the county. In 1859 they welcomed their third child, William, into the family and we find them on the 1861 census living in the little village of Chartham Hatch. By 1871 they have moved to Marden, eight miles south of Maidstone, and two more children have been born. James was still a station master and young William Pett Ridge was at The Marden School. The school has since been rebuilt, with the original building now forming part of the Memorial Hall. Pett

Ridge continued his education at night school in London, at the college now called The Birkbeck Institute.

In 1881 the family were living in Florence Road, Deptford. Four children are still at home, including William, who was working with his brother as a railway clerk and was now listed as 'William P Ridge'.

It was while he was still working at The Railway Clearing House that Pett Ridge began to write. In 1891 his sketches were accepted by the St James Gazette, among others, under the pen name Warwick Simpson.

He wrote over 60 books, which were hugely popular, and at one time it was common opinion that his work would stand the test of time and be rivalled only by that of Charles Dickens. His first novel, *A Clever Wife* was published in 1895, but his popular success came three years later with his novel *Mord Em'ly* (Maud Emily). The portrait of working class life and dialect was considered a triumph. The book was similar to those produced by other authors dubbed The Cockney Novelists, who described working-class life in detail, made palatable with a veneer of wit and stoicism. Even his gravestone shows the connection, dubbing him a 'novelist and friend of the Cockneys'.

Mord Em'ly was adapted into a film in the 1920s, as were three other books, and cemented his view of the Cockney man as a chirpy character and the Cockney woman as a feisty temptress. Pett Ridge was something of a celebrity, mixing with the likes of Mark Twain, and such was his reputation that when he was introduced as 'the Mark Twain of England' he riposted that Twain was 'the Pett Ridge of America'.

Pett Ridge was an enthusiastic supporter of charities involved with the welfare of children, and it is said that he founded a babies' home in Hoxton in 1907. He was a school manager (what we would call a Governor today) and a prison visitor.

Pett Ridge was married in 1909 to Olga, a woman twenty years his junior, with whom he had a son and a daughter. The family lived for five years in a house called Mead View in Green Lane, Chislehurst, and then moved to Ampthill at 3 Willow Grove Villas, Willow Grove on the outskirts of the village.

It was at about this time that he produced a pamphlet called 'In Summer Time' asking for donations towards a project which aimed to purchase Petts Wood in memory of William Willett the instigator of Daylight Saving Time. A memorial now stands in Petts Wood, which is permanently set at Daylight Savings Time. The Daylight Inn in Pett Wood is named after Willett, as is Willett Way.

Pett Ridge died, aged 71, in 1930. He is buried with his wife in St Nicholas' churchyard with the inscription noted above.

Sadly, the author is all but forgotten. From a glittering life-style, in which he rubbed shoulders with HG Wells, JM Barrie, Edith Nesbit, Jerome K Jerome, to name but a few, he has all but disappeared. It has been suggested that his good humoured almost stereotypical character did not fit with the new post-war realism. His chirpy cockney sparrow was replaced with a more gritty representation of the East End population.

40

Christina Rossetti

(1830-1894)

The poetry of Christina Georgina Rossetti is still popular today and continues to be republished.

The poem that most of us would recognise is 'InThe Bleak Midwinter', which was written in Birchington, where she was visiting her brother, who lived in Westcliff Bungalow, Shakespeare Road. Her brother, the artist and poet Dante Gabriel Rossetti, was suffering from Bright's disease. The illness affected his kidneys and as a result he had suffered a stroke, which had left him partially paralyzed. Rossetti stayed with him and nursed him through his final illness. He is buried in the churchyard of All Saints church in the town by the south porch. After this, she wrote the less well-known poem 'Birchington Churchyard', dated 1882.

His passing is recorded by a memorial window in the church, known as The Rossetti Window which was commissioned by his mother. It was designed by his friend Frederick Shield and was inspired by one of Rossetti's own paintings.

After first being used as a Red Cross hospital during The First World War, and then as an air raid shelter, the bungalow was demolished.

Her poem *Birchington Churchyard* talks about:

> "A lowly hill which overlooks a flat,
> Half sea, half country side;
> A flat-shored sea of low-voiced creeping tide
> Over a chalky, weedy mat."

The poem 'In The Bleak Midwinter', originally published under the title 'A Christmas Carol', is also claimed by local residents to have been inspired by Birchington – in particular the railway bridge. It was published in 1872.

> "In the bleak mid-winter
> Frosty wind made moan;
> Earth stood hard as iron,
> Water like a stone;
> Snow had fallen, snow on snow,
> Snow on snow,
> In the bleak mid-winter
> Long ago."

Rossetti did seem to have a soft spot for the county, however, and wrote "One day in the country is worth a month in town".

41

Siegfried Sassoon

(1886-1967)

Siegfried Loraine Sassoon was born in Matfield in West Kent and many of his books refer to his life as a privileged young man, which was brought to an end when he was called-up to serve in the army during World War I at the age of 27. After the war, he returned to Kent and some of his work was completed at his childhood home. Although he soon married and settled in Wiltshire his earlier works present a view of a particular side of Kentish life.

Sassoon grew up in a large old house called Weirleigh in Paddock Wood Road, described by estate agents as a 'neo-gothic mansion'. Sassoon was fond of the house, and echoes of his time there can be found in his later poems, which are more reflective. The ghost of his mother is still said to haunt the building.

Sassoon went to The New Beacon prep school in Sevenoaks, where we can see his name listed in the 1901 census, aged 14.

The poet Robert Graves visited Weirleigh after the war and the house is described in his autobiography *Good-bye to All That* published in 1929. Sassoon was apparently unhappy about Graves' use of his family and their home as inspiration for the book, particularly those parts which described Sassoon's mother and her attempts to contact her dead son via a medium.

His links with Kent are shown in his poetry as a sense of place and a link to the environment, but are particularly strong in 'The Weald of Youth', written in 1942, in which he presages some of the changes that will befall his beloved county. He writes at length about some of his favourite leisure pursuits, including golf at Lamberhurst, cricket at Tunbridge Wells, where he played for the Blue Mantles, and most particularly about hunting. Shades of Kent are also seen in *The Sherston Trilogy.*

His poem 'The Old Century' is also full of his memories of Kent as he looks back on a different way of life.

42

William Shakespeare

(1564-1616)

Playwright and actor Shakespeare was born in Stratford-upon-Avon in 1564, and apart from a few written records, very little is known about this man who is perhaps one of the most famous in the world – even the authorship of his plays is disputed.

We know he travelled widely, and if he travelled to the continent that almost certainly meant a crossing from Dover so it seems very likely that he did stay in the town. The White Cliffs feature in *King Lear* and the Shakespeare Cliff is still a draw for visitors to the area.

In the play Edgar takes the blinded nobleman Gloucester to Dover and pretends that they are standing on the cliff-top.

> "Come on, sir. Here's the place. Stand still. How fearful
> And dizzy 'tis to cast one's eyes so low!
> The crows and choughs that wing the midway air
> Show scarce so gross as beetles. Halfway down
> Hangs one that gathers samphire—dreadful trade!
> Methinks he seems no bigger than his head.
> The fishermen that walk upon the beach
> Appear like mice. And yon tall anchoring bark,"

This scene shows a first-hand knowledge of Kent in two ways, firstly, the mention of choughs, three of which are on the coat-of-arms of Canterbury city, and secondly, the description of the samphire-gatherers, who abseiled from the top of the cliff down onto the cliff-face to collect the plant which grew there – a dangerous occupation without modern climbing equipment, and on a crumbling cliff-edge, too.

We also know that Shakespeare went to Greenwich Palace, then in Kent, as his name appears on a list of players who performed there for Elizabeth I. Another town that he may have been to is Maidstone, where John Burbage, leader of the troupe, 'and his fellows' are known to have stayed.

Of course, Shakespeare did not necessarily visit all the places mentioned in his plays, but we have to consider that he may have made his way along the north coast of Kent at least as far as Chatham, to see The Royal Dockyard.

In King *Henry IV Part 2*, Prince Hal and Falstaff are seen at Gad's Hill, described by Daniel Defoe as a place that was 'noted for robbers of seamen after they have received their pay at Chatham.'

Perhaps the most teasing hint that Shakespeare came to and possibly stayed in Kent is the play 'Arden of Feversham', written in *1592* although and even after 500 years, nobody knows the name of the playwright. Many people think it was William Shakespeare, or a collaboration between Shakespeare, Marlow, and (possibly) other authors. One thing is certain: a man called Thomas Arden did live in Faversham, and was murdered by his wife and her lover. The crime happened in 1551, and it has been widely repeated in documents of the day and in books like *The Newgate Calendar* (a work of 1795 which was the 19th century equivalent of a docu-drama).

The plot of the play is simple, and faithfully follows the facts of the case: Alice Arden wanted to get rid of her husband so she could marry her lover Richard Mosby. The events unfold like a black comedy, with Arden refusing the drink the poisoned milk he was offered, and surviving a strangling attempt, a blow to the head and a cut throat, before being stabbed to death. Concealing the body in a cupboard while entertaining guests, a botched attempt to hide the corpse and a trail of bloody footprints make the whole affair seem like a farcical comedy sketch, but Arden was murdered, and his killers were eventually brought to justice.

We know that Shakespeare often drew on historical stories for his plots, and London is not so far from Faversham. Perhaps he did collaborate with Kentish man Kit Marlow, or with another playwright. Scholars point to the many linguistic similarities to Shakespeare's work, not least the reference to Alice Arden trying to scrub the blood from her floor "The blood cleaveth to the ground and will not out". There is even a character called Shakebag in the play! The killer of poor Thomas Arden was found, but unless further evidence comes to light, the author of the play 'Arden of Feversham' may never be discovered.

And finally, Shakespeare pays a compliment to the men of Kent County. In *King Henry VI part 2,* he writes:

> "Kent, in the Commentaries Caesar writ,
> Is termed the civilist place of all this isle,
> Sweet is the country because full of riches,
> The people liberal, valiant, active, wealthy,"

Which, although ascribed to Julius Caesar, may well be the opinion of the author himself.

Arden's House, Faversham

43

W Somerset Maughham

(1874-1976)

Having lived with his parents in France for the first ten years of his life, the author William Somerset Maugham came to Kent when the death of his mother was quickly followed by that of his father. He came to live with the Rev Henry Maugham, Vicar of Whitstable, who was his uncle.

The residents of Whitstable are quick to claim kinship with the writer, but it appears that he himself was not happy while he lived in Kent, either at home in Whitstable, or at school in Canterbury.

The vicarage in which he grew up has now been demolished, and it seems that he would not have been sorry to hear this. All Saints Church, where his uncle was the incumbent still stands, and young Maugham would have attended services each Sunday.

Accounts of life in Whitstable have found their way into his work, and the town appears as 'Blackstable' in *Of Human Bondage* and in *Cakes and Ale*.

Maugham was soon sent to board at The Kings School in Canterbury, a mere six miles from Whitstable. His time at the school was not much happier than that in Whitstable. His first language was French, and he spoke with a strong French accent. Due to this, coupled with his lack of stature and his natural shyness, he developed a stammer, which led to further misery. Canterbury can be recognised in *Of Human Bondage* as the town Tercanbury.

It does, however, it seems that his feelings for the school mellowed over time and in 1953 he paid for a new boat-house to be built at Pluck's Gutter on the River Stour near Grove Ferry. He also provided funds for a new science building and a library room, as well as donating a complete collection of his works.

The final act which shows his forgiveness was that after his death his ashes were scattered in the school grounds. A plaque marks the event.

44

Rosemary Sutcliff

(1920-1992)

Rosemary Sutcliff was born in Surrey, and was diagnosed with Still's Disease at an early age. The family soon moved to Malta, where they spent almost five years. Her children's books are still in print and many have been made into TV productions and films.

On their return to the UK, the Sutcliffs lived for a while in Sevenoaks, then, in 1926, her father was offered a post as King's Harbour Master at Sheerness Dockyard, on the Isle of Sheppey, and they moved there. Sutcliff was sent to Miss Amelia Beck's school for the children of naval officers where she met other children and caught up on the schoolwork she had missed as a youngster.

It was while they lived on the bleak island, in a cottage in Dockyard Terrace, Sheerness, that she began to love the open countryside and marshland that appeared in so many of her books.

Two years later, Mr Sutcliff was posted to West Africa and Sutcliff and her mother stayed in England, moving to Westgate, just outside Margate. Here they had the benefit of the sea air and possibly the use the facilities at The Sea Bathing Hospital. They stayed for 18 month, until Mr Sutcliff returned in 1930 and the family moved to Chatham.

Sutcliff was a prolific writer and her best-known book, *The Eagle of the Ninth* was published in 1954. She continued to write about Roman Britain, taking inspiration from both Richborough and The Romney Marsh, where the novel *Outcast* is set. She never married and died in West Sussex at the age of 72.

45

W M Thackeray

(1811-1863)

Vanity Fair author William Makepiece Thackerary was first introduced to Tunbridge Wells in the 1820s when he came to the town for his summer holidays. The family stayed in a cottage on the common and he used his memories of the town in *The Virginians.*

Returning as an adult in 1860, he stayed at Rock Villa which has since been renamed Thackeray's House. This is where he wrote *Tunbridge Toys*, which was serialised in The Cornhill Magazines as part of The Roundabout Papers. He mentions Tunbridge Common, overlooked by the rocks, and the sight of children playing cricket there. He talks about the library and the shops in The Pantiles which sell Tunbridge Ware, but is saddened to find that forty years later they are much changed. He was not, I am sure, sad to have left behind the frightened little boy who was left alone in the creaking house while his parents went to town.

Whilst travelling through the county on his way to Belgium, Thackeray stopped at Canterbury. He went to the cathedral, where he spent an hour and wrote afterwards of the "most charming, harmonious, powerful combination of shafts and arches – beautiful whichever way you saw them developed like a fine music or the figures in a kaleidoscope rolling out mysteriously". However, he also called it a "grand, soaring, artificial building" and gave the opinion that a simpler design might aid contemplation while at prayer.

He was miserable in Dover, as he had a "long, dismal, rainy day" utterly to himself and "the blue devils – that is to an extreme melancholy and unwillingness to work".

Thackeray used a further location in Kent, Margate, as his setting for his last, unfinished, work, *A Shabby Genteel Story*, about an impoverished gentleman taking a cheap out-of-season lodging in Margate. This indicates that he may also have ventured further east into the county.

46

Edward Thomas

(1878-1917)

The poet Philip Edward Thomas moved from London to Bearsted with his wife and son in 1901. They lived firstly in Rose Acre Cottage, a mile outside the centre of the village, which they considered to be damp and dismal. At the time, Thomas earnt his living as a critic, reviewing the work of other writers, and taking long walks when time allowed. On one occasion he walked as far as Staplehurst, 12 miles away.

One of his great passions was his garden. The cottage came with an acre of land, which he intended to overhaul completely. He writes in February 1902 of the snowdrops in his garden, and how the garden keeps him going from month to month. Flowers had an important role in his life, bringing solace through his darker moods, featuring in the folk tales he collected, and singing from the lines of his poetry. His pastoral imagery takes inspiration from several sources, and mixes memories from many of the places he lived. Two poems, 'Tears' and 'May 23' reference hops, and we might hope that this means he remembers his time in Kent with pleasure.

They lived in the cottage for two years, before moving to Ivy Cottage (now Ivy House) on The Green in 1903. The cottage is now hidden under the new Roseacre Estate.

After a year in Ivy Cottage, they once more moved, this time to Else's Farm, on the outskirts of Sevenoaks Weald in Morley's Road. Thomas described the view from his upstairs window in the poem 'The Long Small Room'. During his time at the house, he published a series of four essays that he had written at Rose Acre Cottage, known as The Rose Acre Papers. To maintain an income, he also wrote guidebooks and folk tales.

Through his work, Thomas had come into contact with Welsh poet W H Davies, and Davies moved onto Else's farm near the family, renting a cottage from them.

Thomas only lived at the farm for two years, but it made a lasting impression on him and the farm featured in *The Heart of England*, one of the works which became known as his 'country books'.

Thomas moved to Hampshire in 1906. He never returned to Kent, as he was tragically killed in 1917, aged 38, at The Battle of Arras.

47

Russell Thorndike

(1885-1972)

Actor and writer Arthur Russell Thorndike was born into a religious family, as his father was a priest in the Anglican Church. The family lived for many years at 2 Minor Canon Row in the precincts of Rochester Cathedral.

After attending school in Windsor, Thornkike went to The Kings School in Rochester. He loved Kent and was particularly fond of Dymchurch, where his mother owned a cottage, and he was a frequent visitor. His stories of Dr Christopher Syn, vicar by day and swashbuckler by night, were inspired by the bleak countryside of the Romney Marsh, although they were not necessarily written while he was resident in the area. Legend has it that he and his sister Sybil were unable to sleep one night, while a thunderstorm raged, and the tale of Dr Syn took shape as they invented stories to divert their thoughts. Romney Marsh, with its open, windswept flats and history of smuggling was the ideal setting for the tales.

Based in the 18th century, and drawing on the legends of local smugglers and their struggles with the Riding Officers, the stories grew into a book and were first published in 1915 under the title *Dr Syn: A Tale of the Romney Marsh*. Six more books about Dr Syn and his alias Cap'n Clegg or 'the scarecrow' followed. Many of the names in the book can be found on the gravestones of the local churchyard, giving rise to the theory that Thorndike had found them there, pulling the book even further into that divide between fact and fiction. Similar in character to Robin Hood in his protection of the poor, Dr Syn works from The Ship Inn, in Dymchurch, which is known for its underground passages.

The stories have never lost their popularity and have given rise to a bi-annual Day of Syn, a swashbuckling festival which raises money for local charities. 'The Scarecrow' is, of course, present, along with many dragoons, pirates and highwaymen engaging in mock battles and parades, all supported by a selection of folk music and Morris dancing. Fans can also see the larger-than-life character in the films made in 1937, 1962 and 1963.

Thorndike died in Norfolk, aged 87, but is buried in St Peter and St Paul's Churchyard in Dymchurch.

Rochester Cathedral

48

Mary Tourtel

(1874-1948)

The illustrator Mary Caldwell was born in Canterbury and attended the Simon Langton Grammar School for Girls. She stayed in the area and studied art at The Sidney Cooper School of Art, which operated in the building now known as The Beaney House of Art and Knowledge, and she was in fact taught by the great man himself. Tourtel lived at 52 Palace Street with her parents.

After completing her education, Mary found work as a professional book illustrator and in 1900 married Henry Tourtel, sub-editor of The Daily Express.

As luck would have it, The Daily Express was looking for a strip cartoon to rival that in another paper, and Mary and Henry worked together, he writing and she drawing, to produce 'Little Lost Bear'. The first cartoon appeared in November 1920 and ran every day thereafter.

The original brown bear was usually to be seen wearing a blue jumper and cream trousers, but soon changed to the white bear in the red and yellow outfit we now recognise so readily as Rupert.

Mary continued to draw the Rupert cartoons until 1935, when, in her mid-60s, her eyesight began to fail. She died aged 74 at The Kent and Canterbury Hospital in the town she had lived in all her life. She is buried in St Martin's Church, overlooking the city.

Queens Lodgings, Canterbury

49

HG Wells

(1866-1946)

Science fiction giant Herbert George Wells was born in Bromley, which was at the time still part of the county of Kent. As with many other writers, he drew on his earliest memories, and Bromley becomes Bromstead in *The New Machiavelli* (1911).

Wells lived for a time at 23 Eardley Road, Sevenoaks with his girlfriend at the time and her mother. It was here that he wrote *The Time Machine* (1894) which is widely recognised as the first English language sci-fi story, that is, a fictional story based on scientific theories of the time.

Wells moved to Sandgate in 1896, when he was 30. He and his wife rented firstly Beach Cottage, on the corner of Granville Road East and Granville Parade, and then Arnold Place, 20 Castle Road. They liked the town so much that they commissioned acclaimed architect CF Voysey to design and build a new home for them in the area.

Spade House, in Radnor Cliff Crescent became the couple's permanent home, and it was here that they brought up their two sons. The name of the house came from the shape of a spade over the front door. Voysey usually 'signed' his buildings with a heart over the door, but Wells asked for the symbol to be changed to that of a spade instead.

The War of the Worlds was published in 1897, and Deal and Broadstairs are mentioned briefly, if only to illustrate the possible spread of destruction outwards from London.

While living in Spade House, Wells wrote the autobiographical novel *Kipps* (1905), as well as *The First Men in the Moon* (1900), about the adventures of a scientist living in Lympne. *The War in the Air* (1907) which also starts in Kent, and *The Sea Lady (*1899*)*, draws on the towns of both Sandgate and Folkestone for inspiration.

The house is now a retirement home, and has been renamed Wells House.

Wells left the area in 1909, but not before it gave inspiration for other stories. The novel *The History of Mr Polly* is set in the fictional town of Fishbourne, and which bears a striking similarity to Sandgate.

Kipps also has many Kentish links, not so subtly disguised. Kipps is raised by an uncle and aunt who have a shop in New Romney, he then undertakes an apprenticeship at a drapery shop in Folkestone, and eventually opens a bookshop in Hythe. The book was the basis for the popular musical *Half a Sixpence*, starring Tommy Steele.

Another link with Kent is shown in *The Red Room* (1894), in which the narrator devises a rhyme "Ingoldsby-style", showing that the legends of Richard Barham were known to Wells.

The area remembers him fondly, and there is an HG Wells festival in Folkestone in September each year.

Maunsell Sea Forts near Whitstable

50

William Wordsworth

(1770-1850)

Although permanently resident in the North of England, William Wordsworth would have passed through Kent several times during his lifetime, on his way to and from Europe. He travelled to and from Dover at least twice, in 1802 and again in 1820.

He also holidayed in the county for longer periods on occasion. One trip to Dover brought back memories of his travels across The English Channel in 1802, when he had written 'Composed in the Valley Near Dover, on the Day of Landing'

> "Dear fellow Traveller! here we are once more.
> The Cock that crows, the Smoke that curls, that sound
> Of Bells, those Boys that in yon meadow-ground
> In white sleev'd shirts are playing by the score,
> And even this little River's gentle roar,
> All, all are English. Oft have I look'd round
> With joy in Kent's green vales; but never found
> Myself so satisfied in heart before."

and 'Near Dover'.

" Inland, within a hollow vale, I stood;
And saw, while sea was calm and air was clear,
The coast of France,—the coast of France how near!"

It appears he was not happy in Dover "as to Dover not only the winds, but the saline air, the white cliffs and dazzling waters are all enemies that I am afraid of".

In 1820 he once again travelled to the continent, and once again wrote two poems on his return, 'At Dover' and 'After Landing – the Valley of Dover'.

In 1823, he stayed with his wife stayed for five weeks at Strawberry Hill, Dartford, the home of his publisher's son.

Wordsworth stayed in Broadstairs in 1837, when he was 67, leaving his wife at home in The Lake District. He brought with him his daughter Dora, whose doctors had recommended a period of recuperation near the sea after an illness.

The party travelled from London to Gravesend by steamboat, and then took an omnibus to Chatham Docks, where they stayed for a few days with Wordsworth's cousin. Dora, in fact, extended her stay in Chatham while Wordsworth continued on to Broadstairs. He had intended to meet an acquaintance in Canterbury before travelling on to the coast, but the coaches were delayed and Wordsworth, finding his friend has left already, was forced to stay the night in Canterbury. He visited the cathedral, and expressed the desire to see Lee Priory, a country house between Bramling and Littlebourne, which he would have done if it had been closer.

An early morning call at 4am woke Wordsworth for the coach to Ramsgate, where he hired a fly to take him on to Broadstairs, arriving a little before 8am at 5 Prospect Place, where he was staying with poet Samuel Rogers. Rogers. Wordsworth wrote to Dora " This is a very pleasant, though not particularly amusing place; but the drives are agreeable; yesterday I went with Rogers to Margate and Kingsgate but it rained so we could not get out of the Carriage."

In all, Wordsworth spent a week at Broadstairs, also going to Margate and Ramsgate. Of Ramsgate, he wrote to Dora that she would prefer it to Broadstairs because it was "'much more amusing on account of the size of the harbour, the fine quays or piers, and the multitude of vessels".

He only stayed a week in Thanet, after which he took the steam packet from Margate back to Gravesend, to see Dora again before returning home.

To The Men Of Kent – October 1803

Vanguard of Liberty, ye men of Kent,
Ye children of a Soil that doth advance
Her haughty brow against the coast of France,

Now is the time to prove your hardiment!
To France be words of invitation sent!
They from their fields can see the countenance
Of your fierce war, may ken the glittering lance
And hear you shouting forth your brave intent.
Left single, in bold parley, ye, of yore,
Did from the Norman win a gallant wreath;
Confirmed the charters that were yours before;–
No parleying now! In Britain is one breath;
We all are with you now from shore to shore:–
Ye men of Kent, 'tis victory or death!

Dover Castle

Printed in Great Britain
by Amazon

69150475R00098